W9-AFZ-849

THE STRANGER

on the Road to Emmaus

WORKBOOK

JOHN R. CROSS

Published by GOODSEED® International

Scripture quotations are taken from the Holy Bible, New International Version®. NIV®. Copyright ©1973, 1978, 1984 by the International Bible Society. Used by permission of Zondervan Publishing House.

Scripture quotations taken from the HOLY BIBLE,
NEW INTERNATIONAL VERSION.
Copyright © 1973, 1978, 1984 by International Bible Society.
Used by permission of Hodder & Stoughton Limited.
All rights reserved.

"NIV" is a registered trademark of the International Bible Society.
UK trademark number 1448790

THE STRANGER ON THE ROAD TO EMMAUS–WORKBOOK
EDITION 4a

Copyright © 2008 by GOODSEED® International

GOODSEED® International
P.O. Box 3704
Olds, AB   T4H 1P5
Canada

'GOODSEED,' and the Book/Leaf design mark
are trademarks of GOODSEED International.

ISBN 978-1-890082-56-7

All rights reserved. No portion of this book may be reproduced in any form without the written permission of the copyright holder.

Printed in USA   200809-085-15000

*I would like to express appreciation to
Meredith DeRidder for pioneering this
WORKBOOK, to my daughter Naomi for
taking it the next great leap forward,
and to my wife Janice, and my brother David
for giving it the final polish.*

CONTENTS   REVIEW QUESTIONS

TAKE TIME TO READ THIS ...

The thought of studying the Bible can be intimidating. It's a big book. It's also a controversial book. One could wonder if there is any hope of understanding it. But be encouraged, it is not as time consuming as one might think to master the Bible's core message. Many people watch more hours of TV in one week than it takes the average person to complete this study. Now here are a few pointers before you begin:

1. Learn for the sake of *knowing* for yourself. The point of this book is to study the main theme of the Bible. Whether you believe it or not is up to you. There is no need to argue your present beliefs or future conclusions.

2. Get the big picture first. Don't impede the study's momentum. Unless it is a question needed to clarify subject material being studied, write your query down and save it till the end. Once you have the big picture in mind, you can go back and fill in the details by getting your questions answered.

3. Learn one section at a time, in the sequence it is written. This is not the type of Bible study where you can jump around from one lesson to another. It is important that you read each chapter section in THE STRANGER and answer the questions in this WORKBOOK first, **before** you move on to the next section. If you answer a question incorrectly, look it up on the page as indicated and briefly review the material. It will only take a minute, but it will help you immensely as you study deeper into the book. Be alert for those questions that may appear from content studied in previous sections.

    If stopping and answering the questions in this WORKBOOK seems to disrupt the flow of the story in your mind, then set it aside and just read THE STRANGER.

4. Make sure you complete the study. To make a final judgment about the Bible's primary message before finishing the study, entails a high risk of drawing wrong conclusions.

... continued

5. The questions in this *WorkBook* should **not** be viewed as an exam or test. They are *review questions* only—to help you make sure you have a grip on the key points. Don't be insulted if you find a question too easy—it means you understand the material. Others may find it hard. Some of them can be a little tricky! In a number of instances, more than one answer is right. Mark all that are correct. For *fill in the blank* questions, the number of letters in the word are indicated by the line spaces.

6. The content under the label, FOR FURTHER CONSIDERATION, not only reinforces what you have learned, but helps develop Bible navigation skills.

7. To maximize your comprehension, you also need:

   a) A Bible: You can do the whole study without one, but for best results obtain a Bible that has both the Old and New Testaments. Since the optional verses appearing in the sections titled, FOR FURTHER CONSIDERATION, are taken from the Bible translation called the NEW INTERNATIONAL VERSION® NIV®, we would suggest you consider obtaining a copy of that translation.

   b) THE STRANGER ON THE ROAD TO EMMAUS: This book includes approximately 1300 Bible verses quoted with accompanying commentary. Though it's your study guide, it reads like a storybook, not a textbook. If you don't have this book, see the back page to order a copy. The WORKBOOK answers are keyed to this book.

Now open THE STRANGER ON THE ROAD TO EMMAUS, read the Preface on page 1, and begin with Chapter One.

Enjoy your study!

What the Bible says about God:

Blessed are they who … seek him with all their hearts. PSALM 119:2

… he who comes to God must believe that He is, and that He is a rewarder of those who diligently seek Him. HEBREWS 11:6

CHAPTER ONE
REVIEW QUESTIONS

1 PROLOGUE

2 GETTING THINGS STRAIGHT

3 A UNIQUE BOOK

1 PROLOGUE

There are no questions on this section.

2 GETTING THINGS STRAIGHT

1. The Bible is the oldest and longest-standing best seller.

    ☒ True

    ❑ False

2. In many ways, the Bible is like a puzzle—to understand it accurately, the pieces must be put together in the right way.

    ☒ True

    ❑ False

3. Excellent keys for gaining an understanding of the Bible are: (Remember to mark *all* that are true.)

    A. Learn the simple concepts first, then move to the more complex.

    B. Start at the beginning and then study it in the order of events which are said to have happened.

    C. Stick to one theme at a time.

    D. Get the big picture in mind, then if you wish, go back and fill in the details.

4. The Bible addresses many different subjects and themes. If you randomly mix these themes or subjects together, the result will be:

    A. a clear understanding of the Bible

    B. confusion

5. The stated goal of *THE STRANGER ON THE ROAD TO EMMAUS* is to:

    A. cover key biblical events.

    B. enhance understanding by stringing the Bible's stories together in logical sequence.

    C. give one an extensive and comprehensive understanding of the Bible.

    D. tie the biblical stories together into one continuous and clear message.

3   A UNIQUE BOOK

1. The Bible is a collection of *how many* different books?

    A. 44

    B. 55

    C. 66 ✓

2. How many people did God use to write these books?

    A. Twelve people

    B. More than forty people ✓

    C. About 1500 people

3. How many years did it take to write the entire Bible?

    A. Approximately 5000 years

    B. 70 years exactly

    C. Approximately 1500 years ✓

4. According to the Scripture, who was the author of every book in the Bible?

    A. A single human prophet

    B. God ✓

    C. The Bible does not say.

5. The Bible says that God and his words are inseparable, which is one reason the Bible is often referred to as:

    A. God's Word. ✓

    B. Scripture.

6. The Bible says that God guided the prophets in such a way that what was recorded was precisely what he wanted written. As necessary, they could add related thoughts.

    ❏ True

    ❏ False ✓

7. We have ample reason to be assured that the Bible we have today is _____ what the prophets wrote.

    A. essentially the same as ✓

    B. radically different than

    C. somewhat similar in the essentials to

8. The Scripture can be divided into three parts—the Old Testament, the New Testament and the Concordance.

    ☑ True

    ❑ False

9. What significant claim does the Bible make about itself in relation to God?

    A. It gives man's ideas about what God is like.

    B. It is God's message to man.

FOR FURTHER CONSIDERATION:

1. In ancient times, a prophet was a messenger who passed on God's words to the people. The message usually addressed aspects of daily living, but almost invariably, the prophet's message included things yet to come. This foretelling of the future had a practical aspect to it. It was a potent test to determine whether a prophet was genuine.

   If what a prophet proclaims in the name of the LORD does not take place or come true, that is a message the LORD has not spoken.   *DEUTERONOMY 18:22*

   A prophet's message was validated by the accurate fulfillment of his prophecies. He had to be 100% correct—there was no room for error.

   "But a prophet who presumes to speak in my name anything I have not commanded him to say, or a prophet who speaks in the name of other gods, must be put to death.   *DEUTERONOMY 18:20*

   In other words, a prophet had to be 100% right or he was dead. Obviously such a system discouraged "would be" false prophets.

2. Find the beginning and end of the Old and New Testaments.

3. Identify those parts of the Bible which are *not* God's Word, such as footnotes, Concordance, maps, etc.

4. In a Bible, find and read these verses (BOOK *chapter*:verse):

   2 TIMOTHY 3:16;   2 PETER 1:20,21;   PSALM 119:160

CHAPTER TWO
REVIEW QUESTIONS

1 IN THE BEGINNING GOD

2 ANGELS, HOSTS AND STARS

1   IN THE BEGINNING GOD...

Remember that more than one answer can be correct.

1. The Bible says that God created himself in eternity past.

    ☑ True

    ❑ False

2. The Bible says that God has existed from *everlasting* past and will exist to the _e y e r l a s t i n g_ future.

3. According to the Bible, what does God need to exist?

    A. The basic essentials of all life

    B. Eternal matter

    C. ✓Nothing

4. God has many names which describe his character. One of these is the name _I   AM_, which carries the idea of God being the *self-existent one*. (two words)

5. The name LORD focuses our attention on God's position—He is LORD of lords.

    ☑ True

    ❑ False

6. The term *The Most High* shows that there are very few like Him. He is a ruler over this universe.

    ❑ True

    ☑ False

7. The Bible states that God is *Sovereign*, which means He is the _____ of the Universe.

    A. Lord

    B. Ruler ✓

    C. King

8. The Bible clearly states that there is only _O N e_ God.

9. The Bible says that God is invisible. He is a _S P I R I T_.

FOR FURTHER CONSIDERATION:

In a Bible, find and read these verses (BOOK *chapter*:verse):

PSALM *102*:12;   PSALM *8*:1;   JEREMIAH *10*:10A

2 Angels, Hosts and Stars

1. The Bible calls spirits by different names:
    A. Cherubim
    B. Angels
    C. Stars
    D. Hosts

2. The Bible indicates that angels are:
    A. innumerable
    B. invisible
    C. equal to God

3. Angelic beings were created to serve God.
    ❏ True
    ❏ False

4. Circle the words that most correctly communicate God's relationship with his created beings.

    He who _____ the paddle, also _____ the paddle.

creates	fixes
buys	owns
breaks	sells

5. Though angelic beings are very powerful and intelligent, they do not have the ability to choose because they were not created with a will.
    ❏ True
    ☑ False

6. What was the Latin name used for the most powerful, most beautiful spirit ever created?
    A. Gabriel
    B. Lucifer
    C. Michael

7. The word anointed means *"to set apart for a special task."*

    ☑ True

    ❑ False

8. The Bible states that God is worthy of:

    A. praise╱

    B. nothing

9. The word *worship* means to declare a person's W o r T h .

FOR FURTHER CONSIDERATION:

In a Bible, find and read these verses (BOOK *chapter*:verse):

NEHEMIAH 9:6;   PSALM *145*:3;   REVELATION 4:11

CHAPTER THREE
REVIEW QUESTIONS

1 HEAVEN AND EARTH

2 IT WAS GOOD

3 MAN AND WOMAN

1 Heaven and Earth

1. The first book in the Bible is Genesis which means *beginnings*.
    - ☑ True
    - ❏ False

2. What means did God use to create?
    - A. He used angels.
    - B. ✓He simply spoke.
    - C. He used the basic elements.

3. We as humans, create—but only with pre-existing materials. God created everything out of _N o T h i n g_.

4. God holds unlimited power in the universe not equaled by any other being.
    - ☒ True
    - ❏ False

5. The Bible states that God is an extremely intelligent being but is limited in knowledge.
    - ❏ True
    - ☒ False

6. The Bible maintains that only God possesses this triad of attributes. He is:
    - A. all - _k n o w i n g_.
    - B. all - _p o w e r f u l_.
    - C. everywhere present at _A l l   T i m e s_

7. The Bible clearly teaches the concept of *pantheism*—that God is *in* everything, and everything *is* God.
    - ❏ True
    - ☒ False

For further consideration:

In a Bible, find and read these verses (Book *chapter*:verse):

Psalm *33*:8, 9; Psalm *139*:1-6; Isaiah *40*:25,26,28

2   IT WAS GOOD

(For "fill in the blank" questions, pick the best answer from the Word-Bank below.)

1. The Bible says that it took God seven days to create the world.

    ❏ True

    ☒ False

2. The Scriptures indicate that the world, as originally created, was different from what we now know.

    ❏ True

    ☒ False

3. The whole universe performs according to precise rules, revealing that God is a God of _o r d e r_.

4. Almost instinctively, we treat these natural laws with great respect because we understand that *whenever you have a law, you also have a consequence.*

    ☒ True

    ❏ False

5. God determined that each animal would reproduce according to its _k i n d_, meaning that a cat can only reproduce another cat.

6. The Bible says that, *"God saw that it was good."* In other words, everything He made was:

    A. perfect. ✓

    B. flawless. ✓

    C. pure.

7. God's creation was perfect because perfection is part of his character. Two other words that describe this aspect of the Lord's pure nature are _r i g h t e o u s_ and _h o l y_ both meaning *to be without blemish.*

8. God created the rich variety we see and experience for our enjoyment. God is a God who truly _l o v e s_.

WORD-BANK

holy order kind righteous cares friendly loves trust

FOR FURTHER CONSIDERATION:

Using a Bible, find the book of GENESIS, chapter 1 and review the Days of Creation. Find and match the following:

_e_ Day One	a. vegetation
_g_ Day Two	b. birds
_f_ Day Three	c. God rested
_a_ Day Four	d. land animals, man
_b_ Day Five	e. the expanse (atmosphere)
_d_ Day Six	f. stars
_c_ Day Seven	g. light

3 MAN AND WOMAN

1. The Bible says that man was created in the image of God. In part, this means that God created man with: (Three are correct.)

    A. a mind.

    B. a physical body.

    C. emotions.

    D. a will.

2. Which statement is true?

    A. God breathed life into man.

    B. Man became alive on his own.

    C. An angel brought man to life.

3. What does the name *Eve* mean?

    A. Servant.

    B. Life-giver.

    C. Woman.

4. God placed Adam and Eve in a garden named Eden. This garden was:

    A. just adequate to meet their basic needs.

    B. a luxuriant paradise with overwhelming abundance.

    C. insufficient to meet their desires.

5. God had to ask Adam and Eve's permission before taking any action that would affect them.

    ❏ True

    ☑ False

6. God was Adam and Eve's Creator, therefore he was also their O w n e r.

7. What was the one thing that Adam and Eve were commanded not to do?

    A. Eat of the Tree of Life

    B. Eat of the Tree of Knowledge of Good and Evil ✓

    C. Eat of either tree

    D. There was no such command.

8. The ability to c h o o s e is what distinguishes man from a robot. It makes a relationship genuine.

9. Because we are able to choose, the word obey _____ has meaning and depth.

    A. "enslave"

    B. "coerce"

    C. "obey"

10. The Bible says that mankind was created to reflect God's grandeur—to honor Him as a son honors his father.

    ☑ True

    ❏ False

11. The Creator was a _____ to Adam and Eve.

    A. a close and caring friend ✓

    B. a knowledgeable yet distant instructor

    C. an aloof and indifferent stranger

12. The Scripture teaches us that only perfect people can live in the presence of a perfect God.

    ☑ True

    ❏ False

FOR FURTHER CONSIDERATION:

1. In Papua New Guinea, the culture dictates that *he who creates the paddle also owns the paddle*. In a Bible, find and read these verses that illustrate the Creator-Owner connection:

   I CHRONICLES 29:11-12;   PSALM 24:1,2;   PSALM 47:2

2. Many Bibles have a concordance in the back. This is a tool to help one find a verse. For example, let's say you can remember that God said he would create man in *"his own image,"* but you cannot remember where the verse is found. Try finding this verse using the concordance by looking up the word *"image:"*

   *So God created man in his own **image**, in the **image** of God he created him; male and female he created them.*

CHAPTER FOUR
REVIEW QUESTIONS

1   I WILL

2   HAS GOD SAID?

3   WHERE ARE YOU?

4   DEATH

1 I WILL

1. Lucifer was a powerful angel _____ by God for special responsibilities.

    A. baptized
    B. anointed ✓
    C. christened

2. The Bible records Lucifer saying two words five times:

    " _I_ _will_ ascend to heaven."

    " _I_ _will_ raise my throne above the stars of God."

    " _I_ _will_ sit enthroned on the mount of assembly on the utmost heights of the sacred mountain."

    " _I_ _will_ ascend above the tops of the clouds."

    " _I_ _will_ make myself like the Most High." ISAIAH 14:12-14

3. Lucifer's rebellion was driven by his own _pride_.

4. To God, a proud heart is a self-centered form of _sin_.

5. The Bible says that because of God's holy nature, he cannot tolerate _sin_ in his presence.

6. When God expelled Satan and his followers from Heaven, Satan became a malicious archenemy to God and declared war on all that God stood for.

    ❏ True
    ❏ False

7. How many angels followed Lucifer in his rebellion?

    A. Half
    B. One-third ✓
    C. Three-fourths

8. Lucifer became known by other names—names that reveal aspects of his character. Match two meanings with each name. See page 50 if you have trouble.

    A. Devil ———————— a. adversary

                                     b. false accuser

    B. Satan   c. slanderer

                                       d. enemy

9. The Bible says that God has prepared a place for these rebellious spirits called the _L_A_ke_ of _f_i_r_e_.

FOR FURTHER CONSIDERATION:

In a Bible, find and read these verses:

EXODUS 15:11;   REVELATION 20:10

2   HAS GOD SAID?

1. The Bible tells us that Satan:

    A. is the great deceiver. ✓

    B. is a harmless jokester.

    C. desires to make us genuinely happy.

    D. is a figment of one's imagination.

2. When Satan arrived in the garden, he planted something in Eve's mind that she had never considered—the creature could _____ the Creator.

    A. criticize

    B. question

    C. trust

3. Satan first twisted God's Word to cause Eve to doubt God, then he outright _____ it.

    A. denied

    B. ignored

    C. approved

4. What Adam and Eve did is similar to children playing in the street against their mother's instructions. The disobedient youngsters think they know _better THAN_ *mom* what is safe and fun. Adam and Eve sinned when they felt they knew _better Than_ *God* what was good for them.

5. The Bible says that God considered Adam and Eve's disobedience to be an innocent mistake—a misunderstanding.

   ❏ True

   ❏ False ✓

6. A broken law has consequences. The Scripture teaches us that sin's effects are very costly.

   ☑ True

   ❏ False

7. Adam and Eve sewed fig leaf clothing for themselves and hid from God because they were experiencing an uncomfortable new feeling, called G U I L T.

8. Adam and Eve had a C h o i c e, to obey or not to obey. Though seemingly small, God considers all disobedience to be S i n.

9. Though Adam and Eve's sin hurt their relationship with God, it did not result in any permanent consequences or repercussions.

   ❏ True

   ☑ False

FOR FURTHER CONSIDERATION:

In a Bible, find and read these verses:

JOHN 8:44;   2 CORINTHIANS 11:14;   1 SAMUEL 15:23A

3 WHERE ARE YOU?

1. God knew that Adam and Eve had eaten the forbidden fruit before he talked with them.

   ☑ True

   ❏ False

2. When God found Adam and Eve in the garden, He began the conversation with a Q U E S T I O N.

3. The Lord wanted Adam and Eve to sort out in *their* minds precisely what had happened. *They had disobeyed Him! They had trusted Satan instead of God.*

   ☑ True

   ❏ False

4. Who did Adam blame for his sin? (Two are correct.)

   A. Eve ✔

   B. God ✔

   C. Himself

   D. The snake

5. Who did Eve blame for her sin? (Two are correct.)

   A. Adam

   B. The snake ✔

   C. Herself

   D. God ✔

6. Adam and Eve confessed that they were guilty sinners.

   ❏ True

   ❏ False ✔

7. Adam and Eve's actions affected:

   A. just themselves.

   B. the whole human race. ✔

8. The Bible says that a male child was promised to come through the future offspring of Eve. This male child would free mankind from the consequences of sin. He would be known as:

   A. The Anointed One.

   B. The Promised Deliverer. ✔

   C. The Chosen One.

9. The Bible also states that Satan would temporarily wound the child, but the child would _____ Satan.

   A. fatally crush ✔

   B. seriously injure

   C. help

10. This promise of a *DELIVERER* added another name to the list of terms that reveal God's character. He would be known as the *one who saves* or *THE SAVIOR*.

    ❏ True ✓

    ❏ False

11. Because of Adam and Eve's sin, nothing remained perfect. The earth and everything in it suffered from the effects of a:

    A. drought.

    B. curse. ✓

    C. flood.

12. Just as defying the law of gravity brings broken bones, so violating God's word has ramifications. The most bitter consequence of sin is <u>death</u>.

FOR FURTHER CONSIDERATION:

In a Bible, find and read these verses:

   ECCLESIASTES 12:14; ROMANS 5:12

4 DEATH

1. In the Bible, death implies some sort of *separation*. It can also mean annihilation or non-existence.

    ❏ True

    ☒ False

2. Match the two meanings.

    ___ A. Death of the Body   1. Separation of man's spirit from God

    ___ B. Death to a Relationship   2. Separation of man's spirit from God forever

    ___ C. Death to a Future Joy, The Second Death   3. Separation of man's spirit from his body

3. The Bible says that God is too pure to look on evil; he cannot tolerate wrong.

    ☒ True

    ❏ False

Complete the crossword puzzle using the questions below. Feel free to use a Bible to fill in the verses. If you would prefer not to do the puzzle, then just fill in the blanks.

ACROSS:

1. The Bible says that sin incurs a debt which must be paid by __*d*__ __*e*__ __*a*__ __*t*__ __*h*__.

2. The Bible says that "...*the* __WAGES__ *of* __SIN__ *is death.*"
   2a   2b   ROMANS 6:23

3. Because man sins, he experiences physical death or death of the __body__.

4. Before Adam sinned, God and man had a mutually friendly __relationship__. When Adam and Eve followed Satan in his rebellion, that __relationship__ died.

5. The Bible, speaking of all mankind, says that we are, "_____ *from God and (are) enemies...*" COLOSSIANS 1:21

6. All mankind is condemned to an __physical__ death.

7. Like begets like, so __sinful__ man reproduces __sinful__ man.

DOWN:

1. The Bible says man will "... *die and returns to the* ___**dust**___."
    Psalm 104:29b

2. The Bible says _All_ mankind is "... *dead in ... transgressions*
    2a
    and _Sin_ ."
    2b
    EPHESIANS 2:1

3. God is holy, therefore He is offended by all sin. It is filthy to
    Him. God is _____ against all sin. He will have no part in it.

4. The Bible says man's sins have _separated_ him from God.

5. Sinful man will experience the same punishment as Satan.
    The Bible calls this the _second_ death, probably because it
    occurs after physical death.

6. Because man followed Satan, after death he will live with
    him in the _lake_ of _fire_ , created for Satan
    6a   6b
    and his followers.

FOR FURTHER CONSIDERATION:

Using a Bible, find and complete the following verses.

✻ ROMANS 5:12 *Therefore, just as sin entered the world through*
    _____ *man, and* _____ *through sin, and in*
    this way _____ *came to* _____ *men, because*
    _____ *sinned.*

    Man has a *sin nature*, often called *Adam's nature*. This nature
    is man's *condition*—it's like a sickness. The *symptoms* of that
    condition are acts of sin.

✻ MATTHEW 25:41 *Then He will say to those on his left, "Depart from*
    me, you who are cursed, into the eternal fire _____
    for the _____ *and his angels."*

CHAPTER FIVE
REVIEW QUESTIONS

1   A PARADOX

2   ATONEMENT

3   TWO BY TWO

4   BABEL

1 A PARADOX

For questions on this page, use word bank below.

1. Just as God established physical laws to govern the universe, so there are spiritual ___*laws*___ to govern the relationship between God and man.

2. Centuries ago in the Middle East, when one incurred a debt, a ___*official Certicate*___ of ___*debt*___ was drafted so that the parties involved would not forget the amount payable.

3. The Bible says that on the moral ledger, sin incurs a debt. We are now faced with a law called *"the law of* ___*sin*___ *and* ___*death*___*."*

4. The Bible says *"the soul who sins shall die."*

    ☑ True

    ❏ False

5. According to the Bible, man's sin-debt can be paid in only one way:

    A. Money

    B. Death ✓

    C. Hard Work

6. Man faces a dilemma that has two facets, like opposite sides of the same coin.

    ❖ We have something we don't want:

    a ___*sin*___ nature, with all its consequences.

    ❖ We need something we don't have:

    a ___*perfection*___ / ___*righteousness*___ that allows us to live in God's presence.

WORD-BANK			
debt	sin	virtue	life
death	pride	love	perfection
morality	certificate	laws	righteousness

7. The Bible says that God is *just* which means that, as a judge, he is fair and impartial.

   ☑ True

   ❑ False

8. God revealed a type of love when he created the world, a _Care_ and _Concern_. But then God unveiled a deeper love, an _undeserved_ love. This love is often referred to using the words *grace, mercy, kindness* and *compassion*. (Use the best words.)

   > concern   undeserved   romantic   care   friendly

9. God judges _a ll_ of our sin, whether here during life on earth, or after physical death.

10. God provided a way for man's sin-debt to be paid in order that man may escape the death penalty. God did this because:

    A. he loved those he created. ✓

    B. Satan demanded it.

    C. man deserves it.

11. The Bible states that the same pride that caused Satan to rebel is what will keep us from coming to God for help. The Lord can only help man escape the penalty of death when:

    A. man humbles himself and seeks God's help. ✓

    B. man is content with who he is.

    C. man finds fulfillment in life.

FOR FURTHER CONSIDERATION:

1. Using a Bible, find and read these verses:

   PSALM 96:10;   PSALM 98: 9;   PSALM 101:1

2. Find and complete the following verses:

   ✳ ISAIAH 61:8   *"For I, the LORD, love _____;*
   I hate robbery and _____ (or sin)."

   ✳ 1 PETER 5:5b   *God opposes the _____*
   but gives grace to the _____.

2 ATONEMENT

1. Adam and Eve could do nothing, outwardly or inwardly, to _remove_ the sin problem.

   | transfer | remember | remove | forget | blame |

2. The Bible states that _death_ is the consequence of sin.

3. Adam and Eve had two children named Cain and Abel. They were both born sinless.

   ❏ True

   ☑ False

4. The Scriptures say, *"Without the _____, there is no forgiveness."*

   A. *washing with water*

   B. *shedding of blood* ✓

   C. *shedding of tears*

5. Based on certain future events, God said that he would accept an animal's death in man's place. This process is called:

   A. alteration

   B. cancellation

   C. substitution ✓

6. The death of an animal graphically illustrated what God's _law_ demanded as payment for man's sin.

   A. law

   B. temper

7. God said that the shed blood would make an atonement for sin, which means it would provide a _sacrifice_ for man's sin.

8. Through faith in God, as demonstrated by the death and the atoning blood on the altar, man would:

   A. be forgiven of sin. ✓

   B. find a restored relationship with God. ✓

   C. be considered righteous. ✓

9. Cain's offering was not acceptable because:
    1. he did not have _T r u s t_ or confidence in God's instructions as being trustworthy.
    2. he did not come to God in _G o d_'s way.

10. The Bible also indicates that there was something wrong with Cain's sacrifice. His sacrifice could not shed _b l o o d_.

11. Cain was angry, yet God was gracious and explained to him that if he came the same way _A b e l_ had come, he too would be accepted.

12. The Bible says that Heaven is a perfect place where God lives with man. There is no pain, sorrow, tears, or _d e a t h_.

13. The Bible says that only those who have their names written in the book of _L i f e_ will enter Heaven.

FOR FURTHER CONSIDERATION:

Find and complete the following verses:

❋ LEVITICUS 17:11 *"For the life of a creature is in the _____, and I have given it to you to make _____ for yourselves on the altar; it is the _____ that makes _____ for one's soul."*

❋ HEBREWS 11:4 *By _____ Abel offered God a better _____ than Cain did. By faith, he was commended as a _____ man, when God spoke well of his offerings.*

3   TWO BY TWO

1. Hundreds of years passed but God did not forget his pledge to send *The Promised* _D e l i v e r e r_.

2. The Bible says that as the world's population grew, more put their faith in God than the many who rejected him.
    - ❏ True
    - ☒ False

3. Though the people of Noah's day disregarded the Lord, God _____ their sin. God is grieved by sin.

    A. was unable to do anything about

    B. did not concern himself with

    C. did not overlook

4. Man was living solely for:

    A. others

    B. God

    C. self

5. Man may have had a life that excluded God, but God still held man accountable for sin.

    ☑ True

    ❑ False

6. Why was Noah different from the other men of his day?

    A. He was a righteous man. ✓

    B. He followed God's Word. ✓

    C. He had faith in God. ✓

7. The Bible indicates that Noah brought an animal sacrifice to God, evidence that he recognized the need to have an innocent substitute pay the d e a t h penalty for him.

8. God told Noah to build an ark. Though this boat was very large, it had only one d o o r.

9. Noah's neighbors did not heed his warning about coming judgment. When the time was up, only Noah and his family entered the ark. Noah shut the door.

    ❑ True

    ☑ False

10. Man sometimes threatens and never delivers, but God always keeps His Word.

    ☑ True

    ❑ False

11. Only an all-powerful God could create the flood circumstances.

    ☑ True

    ❏ False

12. The first thing Noah did when he left the ark was:

    A. look around to see if his friends were alive.

    B. build an altar and offer a blood sacrifice to God. ✓

    C. build a house.

FOR FURTHER CONSIDERATION:

1. Find and read this verse:

    2 PETER 3:3-7

2. Using the Concordance in the back of a Bible, try finding this verse by looking up the word *"commanded:"*

    *And Noah did all that the LORD **commanded** him.*

3. Find and complete the following verses:

    ✳ GENESIS 6:9 ... *Noah was a* __righteous__ *man,* __blameless__ *among the people of his time, and he* __walked__ *with* __God__ .

4   BABEL

1. God was pleased with man's idea to stay in one place and build a big city.

    ❏ True

    ☑ False

2. Man wanted to build a tower to bring honor to:

    A. God.

    B. Noah.

    C. himself. ✓

3. It is right to exalt ourselves because we are truly worthy.

    ❏ True

    ☑ False

4. According to the Scriptures, Babel is the first recorded occurrence of an organized re l e g i o n .

5. A definition for the word r e l e g i o n is this: *man's efforts to reach God.*

6. God says that man is lost, and can not find his own way back to a right relationship with God.

   ☑ True

   ❏ False

7. The Bible says that God provided the only *true* way for man to be restored to the Lord when in his mercy he granted man a way to escape the punishment for sin through faith, as evidenced by the b l o o d sacrifice.

   A. substitutionary animal

   B. blood

   C. atoning (covering)

8. God scattered man throughout the world because they refused to heed his commands and follow him.

   ☑ True

   ❏ False

FOR FURTHER CONSIDERATION:

Find and compare these verses:

   GENESIS 9:1;   GENESIS 11:4

CHAPTER SIX
REVIEW QUESTIONS

1 ABRAHAM

2 BELIEF

3 ISAAC

1   ABRAHAM

1. God told Abram to leave his country and move to an unknown land. Because Abram didn't know where he was going, he had to put _____ in God to lead him one day at a time.

   A. faith

   B. trust

   C. confidence

2. God's first promise to Abram was that he would become a great nation. This was good news to Abram because.

   A. he had many children.

   B. though he had no children, God would somehow give him a son.

   C. he knew he deserved this blessing.

3. Through the promises God gave to Abram, God was telling Abram that one of his descendants would be *The Anointed One.*

   ❑ True

   ❑ False

4. Cross out the incorrect answer.

   God said that because of Abram's [*respect for* / *confidence in*] God, righteousness was [*credited to* / *debited from*] Abram's account, offsetting his [*sin-debt* / *bad luck*].

5. When God looked at Abram, he saw him as _B_____ because he believed God, offering the blood sacrifice as an atonement-covering for his sin.

   A. happy or at peace

   B. pure, right or righteous

   C. upset or disturbed

6. Abram found that to gain *a righteousness equal to God's righteousness* all he had to do was trust the Lord, and God provided it.

    ☑ True

    ❏ False

FOR FURTHER CONSIDERATION:

Find and complete the following verses:

✳ GENESIS 12:2, 3 *Four promises God gave Abram:*

1. *"I will make you into a great _____ and I will bless you;"*

2. *"I will make your name _____, and you will be a blessing."*

3. *"I will _____ those who bless you, and whoever curses you I will _____;"*

4. *"…and_____ peoples on earth will be blessed through you."*

✳ GENESIS 15:6 *Abram _____ the Lord, and he _____ it to him as _____.*

2 BELIEF

1. The words *belief, faith, confidence,* and $\underline{TRUST}$ are often used interchangeably.

2. True faith is built on the:

    A. facts. ⌐

    B. way you feel.

3. Abram's *faith* did not stop with mental assent. Because his faith came right from his heart, he staked everything on his belief and obeyed God.

    ☑ True

    ❏ False

4. Relating the following to God, cross out the incorrect words.

    It's not the [~~kind~~ / *amount*] of faith you have, but in [*whom* / ~~what~~] you are placing your faith.

5. Abram's obedience was an attempt to prove to God and to others the genuineness of his faith.

   ❏ True

   ☑ False

FOR FURTHER CONSIDERATION:

Find and complete the following verse:

❋ HEBREWS 11:6   *And without* ___*faith*___ *it is impossible to please God, because anyone who comes to Him must* ___*believe*___ *that He exists and that He rewards those who earnestly seek Him.*

3   ISAAC

1. Abraham had learned that God was utterly trustworthy, so he did just as God requested. He had _____ in God's goodness.

   A. faltering hope

   B. expectant faith ✓

   C. little belief

2. Though Isaac was Abraham's promised son, Abraham obeyed the Lord, because he was convinced that God could choose to raise Isaac from the dead.

   ☑ True

   ❏ False

3. Once he was bound, Isaac could not save himself. He was:

   A. helpless. ✓

   B. hopeless.

   C. unconscious.

4. Even though God had intervened and told Abraham not to kill Isaac, there still was a death.

   ☑ True

   ❏ False

5. The ram was offered as an acceptable—or *perfect*—sacrifice in Isaac's place. The ram was Isaac's:

    A. friend.

    B. pet.

    C. substitute. ✓

6. God was giving Abraham another lesson about his character. God tested Abraham by commanding him to take his only son and sacrifice him on an altar to show him:

    A. that He could be appeased through child sacrifice.

    B. that He was an angry God.

    C. truths concerning *judgment, faith* and *deliverance through a substitute.* ✓

7. Match the best parallel sentences below.

____ A. Just as Isaac was under God's direct order to *die,*

____ B. God did *intervene.*

____ C. An innocent *animal* died

____ D. Just as Abel had offered a sacrifice to die in *his place,*

____ E. Just as God viewed Abel's sacrifice as *acceptable,*

1. God provided a *substitute.*

2. so God saw fit to provide a ram as an *acceptable* sacrifice in Isaac's place.

3. so all mankind is under the sentence of *death.*

4. so the ram had died in *Isaac's place.*

5. in *man's* place.

8. The provision of a substitute was man's idea.

    ❏ True

    ☒ False

9. This story is a vivid illustration of two people coming to God in God's way, believing that His Word was true.

    ☒ True

    ❏ False

FOR FURTHER CONSIDERATION:

Find and complete the following verse:

✳ HEBREWS 11:17,19 By _____faith_____ Abraham, when God tested him, _Abraham took_ Isaac as a _sacrifice_. He who had received the _____ was about to sacrifice his __one__ and only son...

Abraham __believed__ that God could __raise__ the dead, and figuratively speaking, he did __get__ Isaac back from __dead__ .

CHAPTER SEVEN
REVIEW QUESTIONS

1   ISRAEL AND JUDAH

2   MOSES

3   PHARAOH AND THE PASSOVER

1 ISRAEL AND JUDAH

1. Isaac had two sons, Esau and Jacob. Esau was like Cain—doing his own thing, but Jacob was looked upon as *righteous* because he came to God by faith …

    A. ✓... offering a blood sacrifice as an atonement-covering for his sin.

    B. … praying daily.

    C. … being a good, hard-working man.

2. God renewed His pledge to Abraham and Isaac through Jacob, saying that through Jacob's offspring would come *The Promised* D E L I V e r e r.

3. Jacob had a total of thirteen children. The thirteen tribes of Israel are direct descendants of these men and women.

    ☑ True

    ❏ False

4. Jacob blessed his son, Judah, from whom the *tribe of Judah* descended, saying that *The Anointed One* would come from his tribe.

    ☑ True

    ❏ False

5. Jacob's name was changed to Israel, which means *God prevails*. The modern nation of Israel named itself after this man.

    ☑ True

    ❏ False

6. A famine caused Jacob, his sons, and families (70 people) to move to Egypt. Three hundred and fifty years later they numbered:

    A. approximately 2,500 people.

    B. approximately 250,000 people.

    C. approximately 2 ½ million people.

FOR FURTHER CONSIDERATION:

Find and complete the following verse:

✱ GENESIS 28:15 *"I am with you and will watch over you wherever you go, and I will _____ you back to this _____. I will not _____ you until I have done what I have _____ you."*

2 MOSES

1. Pharaoh enslaved the Israelites because:

    A. they wanted to take control of Egypt.

    B. he needed more laborers.

    C. they were growing too numerous and he feared they might turn against Egypt.

2. Forty years after Moses fled Egypt for murdering an Egyptian, God spoke to him from a flaming bush. As Moses approached the bush, God told Moses to remove his shoes because he was standing on holy ground.

    ☑ True

    ❏ False

3. What did God say to Moses from the flaming bush?

    A. Moses would be justly punished for murder.

    B. Moses would help the Israelites escape out of Egypt.

    C. Moses was a gifted man that God needed.

4. What name—meaning *self-existent one*—did God tell Moses to use with the Israelites?

    A. Almighty God

    B. The Most High

    C. I AM

5. The Israelites did not believe Moses as God said they would.

    ❏ True

    ❏ False

FOR FURTHER CONSIDERATION:

Using the Concordance in the back of a Bible, try finding this verse by looking up the word "*name*:"

> ✳ *God said to Moses, "I AM WHO I AM. This is what you are to say to the Israelites: 'I AM has sent me to you.'"*
>
> *"… This is my **name** forever, the **name** by which I am to be remembered from generation to generation."*

3 PHARAOH AND THE PASSOVER

1. Pharaoh ignored God's order to free the Israelites because:

    A. he did not acknowledge the true God and was firmly opposed to anything that required him to do so.

    B. he could not understand Moses and was confused.

    C. he was busy ruling the country.

2. When God told the Israelites that they would be His people, he meant that only Israelites could be accepted by him.

    ❏ True

    ❏ False

3. God taught both the Israelites and the Egyptians that:

    A. he delivers those who trust Him.

    B. he alone is God.

    C. only Israelites could escape God's punishment.

4. Pharaoh refused to acknowledge and obey the Lord, so God brought ten plagues on Egypt, each targeting an Egyptian god.

    ❏ True

    ❏ False

5. God extends *grace* and *mercy* to those who come to God in God's _____.

6. Because God is gracious, it was acceptable to skip a few of the commands concerning the Passover as long as one did it with good intentions.

   ❏ True

   ☑ False

7. If an Egyptian followed all of God's instructions for the Passover because he believed that the Lord was the only true God, then God would *pass over* his house.

   ☑ True

   ❏ False

8. The firstborn lived, but only because an innocent lamb died. The lamb became the firstborn's substitute.

   ☑ True

   ❏ False

9. Match the parallel sentences below having to do with the concept of substitution.

   ___ A. God had accepted Abel

   ___ B. When Abraham offered Isaac as a sacrifice,

   ___ C. With the Passover,

   1. the ram died *in Isaac's place.*

   2. the lamb died *in the place of the firstborn.*

   3. because an animal had died *in his place.*

FOR FURTHER CONSIDERATION:

The last plague was the death of the firstborn. God, however, provided a way of escape. Find the following verses and complete the commands God gave the Israelites:

✳ EXODUS 12:3   "…*each man is to take a* ___lamb___ *for his family, one for each household.*"

✳ EXODUS 12:5-7   "*The animals you choose must be year-old,* ___me___ *without* ___blemish___."

Take care of them until the fourteenth day of the month, when all the people of the community of Israel must _____ them at _____. Then they are to take some of the _____ and put it on the sides and tops of the _____ of the houses where they eat the lamb."

✳ EXODUS 12:22   "Not one of you shall go _out_____ the door of his house until _morning_____."

✳ EXODUS 12:46   "It must be eaten inside one house; take none of the meat outside the house. Do not _break_____ any of the _bones_____."

✣ EXODUS 12.13   "The blood will be a sign for you on the houses where you are; and when I see the _blood____, I will _pass____ _over____ you."

CHAPTER EIGHT
REVIEW QUESTIONS

1 BREAD, QUAIL AND WATER

2 TEN RULES

3 THE COURTROOM

1 BREAD, QUAIL AND WATER

1. The Israelites were content with the Lord's leading.
   - ❏ True
   - ☑ False

2. The Lord provided for their needs by giving them:
   - A. bread.
   - B. meat.
   - C. new clothes.
   - D. water.

3. God told Moses to tell the people to gather only as much bread as they could eat that day. There would be more the next day. God was teaching them that His Word was:
   - A. to be trusted when times were good.
   - B. true and was to be trusted.
   - C. something important for them to consider.

4. The Israelites obeyed and only collected enough bread for one day at a time.
   - ❏ True
   - ☑ False

5. When you consider their huge population, God's provision for the needs of the Israelites was barely adequate.
   - ❏ True
   - ☑ False

6. Circle ALL the words that could fit in the spaces below.

   God was teaching the Israelites that He was _____ and His word was to be _____.

merciful	lenient	disregarded	trusted
gracious	troubled	ignored	kind	obeyed

7. Man does not deserve God's loving care, yet God provides for man in spite of his sin. This *undeserved love* is called *grace*.
   - ❏ True
   - ❏ False

For Further Consideration:

1. Find and complete the following verses:

   ✱ Exodus 34:6   *And he passed in front of Moses, proclaiming, "The LORD, the LORD, the _____ and _____ God, _____ to anger, abounding in _____ and faithfulness..."*

   ✱ Nehemiah 9:19 *Because of your great _____ you did not _____ them in the desert.*

2. Find and read these verses:

   Isaiah 30:18;   Psalm 78:38

2   Ten Rules

1. The one condition necessary for the Israelites to be used of God was stated as:

   *"If you _O b e y_ me fully and keep my covenant, **then** out of all nations you will be my treasured possession."*

2. The people's response to God's proposal, *If you... Then I...,* revealed their feeling of inadequacy to fulfill any condition.

   ❏ True
   ❏ False

3. The Lord had the Israelites bathe with water to illustrate that _____ is important to a holy God.

   | purity of lifestyle   body cleanliness   sanitation |

4. God directed Moses to put a boundary line around the mountain...

   A. to protect man from falling off cliffs.

   B. to show the Israelites where God lived.

   C. to illustrate the separation that exists between a holy God and sinful man.

5. God told the Israelites that if anything was more important than Him in their lives, then they had broken the first rule.

   ☑ True
   ❏ False

6. The Bible says that God does not want man worshipping idols or any other gods because:

   A. no one knows what He looks like.

   B. only God is worthy of worship.

   C. they do not resemble God.

7. Because of *who* God is, even His name should not be used flippantly or irreverently.

   ☑ True

   ❏ False

8. The fifth rule instructs children to _____ their parents.

worship	honor	pray for	educate

9. The Bible likens certain types of anger to:

murder	temper	tantrums	disrespect

10. God knows our outward actions and what takes place in our:

    A. hearts.

    B. minds.

    C. imagination.

11. Anyone who is deceitful or dishonest is following Satan's agenda because Satan is the *father of* lies.

12. God commanded the Israelites not to be envious, greedy or jealous. To break this command is a form of *pride*.

    ☑ True

    ❏ False

13. When God tells man something, one can usually count on it as being true.

    ❏ True

    ☑ False

14. Down through the years, God's expectations for mankind have changed dramatically.

    ❏ True

    ☑ False

15. The Ten Rules made man aware of what the Lord considered sin.

   ☑ True

   ❏ False

FOR FURTHER CONSIDERATION:

1. Find and complete the following verse:

    ✳ ISAIAH 64:6 _____ of us have become like one who is
       _____, and all our _____ acts are
       like _____ rags; we all shrivel up like a leaf,
       and like the wind our _____ sweep us away.

2. Find EXODUS 20. Underline the commands from 1 to 10.

3. Find and read these verses: EZEKIEL 36:23 PSALM 29:2

3 THE COURTROOM

1. The Bible says that in order to be accepted by God, man must obey *how many* of the commandments?

   A. Any four, completely and perfectly

   B. The first eight (the last two are discretionary)

   C. All of them ✓

2. God holds man accountable for *all* of his sin, even the sin of which he is not aware.

   ☑ True

   ❏ False

3. It is possible to keep all of God's commands consistently and perfectly.

   ❏ True

   ☑ False

4. The Ten Commandments have two main objectives:

   A. To silence those who say their lives are good enough to be accepted by God.

   B. To show mankind that we are indeed law-breakers.

   C. To give mankind a list of rules to keep so we can be pleasing to God.

5. Just as a mirror exposes the dirt, so the ten rules expose man's _S_ _I_N_.

6. God gave the Law so *"that through the commandment sin would become* _U_____ *sinful."*

    A. *reasonably*

    B. *utterly*

    C. *somewhat*

7. The Bible says that man is sinful from:

    A. conception

    B. the influence of society

    C. from the age of two years.

8. God directed the Israelites to be *holy*, a word that has to do with God's _____ character.

    A. aloof

    B. critical

    C. perfect

9. The notion that a person's good living and thinking can outweigh his bad, and therefore merit God's acceptance, is totally foreign to the Bible.

    ☑ True

    ❏ False

FOR FURTHER CONSIDERATION:

Find and complete the following verses:

✳ PSALM 14:3 _____ *have turned aside, they have together become corrupt; there is _____ one who does good, _____ even one.*

✳ ROMANS 3:19,20 *Now we know that whatever the _____ says, it says to those who are under the law, so that _____ mouth may be _____ and the _____ world held _____ to God.*

Therefore _____ one will be declared _____ in his sight by _____ the law; rather, through the law we become _____ of sin.

CHAPTER NINE
REVIEW QUESTIONS

1 TABERNACLE

2 UNBELIEF

3 JUDGES, KINGS AND PROPHETS

1 TABERNACLE

1. The Bible states that the first step in approaching God is for man to recognize that he is a _____ sinner.

   > frustrated   helpless   hopeful   capable

2. When the Israelites built the Tabernacle, they were allowed to build it according to their own design.
   - ❏ True
   - ❏ False

3. The Tabernacle was accessible by only one gate.
   - ❏ True
   - ❏ False

4. The Sanctuary was divided into two sections: one-third of the structure formed the *Holy of Holies* and the other two-thirds, the *Holy Place*. What separated the two rooms?
   - A. A large door
   - B. A gold box
   - C. A very thick curtain or veil

5. Write *HH* beside the furniture found in the *Holy of Holies*, *HP* beside those items placed inside the *Holy Place*, and *CY* beside those pieces located outside in the *Courtyard*.
   - A. _____The Bronze Altar
   - B. _____The Ark of the Covenant
   - C. __H__The Basin
   - D. _____The Lampstand
   - E. __H__The Table with the Bread of the Presence
   - F. _____The Atonement Cover or Mercy Seat
   - G. _____The Golden Altar or The Altar of Incense

6. With the Tabernacle completed, the cloud that led the Israelites moved into position over the *Holy of Holies*, signifying God's presence in the midst of his people.

    ☑ True

    ❏ False

7. After entering the one and only gate, the first step to approaching God was to offer a sacrifice on the Bronze Altar.

    ☑ True

    ❏ False

8. According to Leviticus 1:2-5, this sacrifice had to be:

    A. from the herd or the flock.

    B. a male without defect.

    C. presented just inside the entrance to the Tabernacle.

    D. offered with the individual bringing it, laying his hand on the head of the animal.

    E. killed and its blood sprinkled on the altar.

9. In laying hands on the sacrifice, the individual:

    A. showed compassion for the animal.

    B. demonstrated grief.

    C. identified himself with the offering.

10. When the individual placed his __hand__ on the __head__ of the animal he was offering, he was acknowledging that he deserved to die for his own sin and that the animal was his __substitute__.

    | hands blessing leg head substitute advocate |

11. Because death is the penalty for sin, the sacrifice pictured...

    A. ...what was necessary for sin to be forgiven.

    B. ...God's need for a blood sacrifice.

    C. ...Satan getting paid.

12. Aaron, the High Priest, entered the Holy of Holies once a year—never without [*blood* / *water*] which he offered on the [*Golden Altar* / *Atonement Cover*]. This was done on the Day of Atonement.

FOR FURTHER CONSIDERATION:

1. Find and read the following verses:

   EXODUS 40:17-38 PSALM 85:2 PSALM 99:1-3

2. Find and complete the following verse:

   ✻ LEVITICUS 17:11 *"For the ________ of the creature is in the ____________, and I have given it to you to make __________________ for yourselves on the __________; it is the ____________ that makes __________________ for one's __________."*

2 UNBELIEF

1. As the Israelites learned more about the Lord, they also were more __________ for those things they knew.

worthy	accountable	esteemed

2. From the time the Tabernacle was built to the end of their journey, the Israelites were content and thanked God for his provisions.

   ❑ True

   ❑ False

3. God may delay judgment on sin for a period of time, but eventually he judges all sin.

   ❑ True

   ❑ False

4. Judgment came to the Israelites in the form of:

   A. hail.

   B. snakes.

   C. a return to Egyptian slavery.

5. The Bible states that the *"wages of sin is* <u>death</u>*"*

6. God's purpose in judging the Israelites was to bring about a change of attitude—a change of mind. In the Bible, this change is described by the word <u>repent</u>.

7. Only during this life on earth can people repent and be heard by God.

   ☑ True

   ❏ False

8. When an Israelite was bitten by a snake, all he had to do was turn, look at _____ and he would be healed.

   A. Moses

   B. ✓the bronze serpent

   C. his snake bite

9. This one look was a mind-over-matter stratagem.

   ❏ True

   ☑ False

FOR FURTHER CONSIDERATION:

Find and read the following verses:

   NEHEMIAH 9:19-21;   2 KINGS 18:1-6

3   JUDGES, KINGS AND PROPHETS

The diagram below portrays the Israelites' relationship with God during the time of the Judges. Number the four words in the sequence which best illustrates the history of the Israelites.

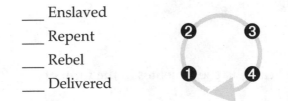

   ___ Enslaved

   ___ Repent

   ___ Rebel

   ___ Delivered

Complete the crossword puzzle using the questions below. Feel free to open chapter Nine and find the answers.

ACROSS:

1. When Moses died he was replaced by _____*Joshua*_____ .

2. The Promised Land was divided into twelve _____ .

3. Before the Israelites had an earthly king, their leader was _____ .

4. Because other countries had _____ as rulers, Israel rejected God and asked for their own.

5. King _____ was a well-known leader of Israel.

6. King _____ completed his father's ambition.

7. Though these Kings were considered spiritual leaders, the Bible still says they were needy, _____ sinners.

8. The temple was built on Mount Moriah, probably on the same location where Abraham offered _____ .

9. After the kingdom split, the ten northern tribes retained the name of _____.

10. During the time of captivity in Babylon, those people from Judah became known as _____.

11. The _____ were Greek-influenced Jews who took away from God's Word.

12. Jewish religious zealots created additional rules that encompassed God's _____ so as to be careful not to break any of God's commands.

13. _____ ____ _____ was appointed by the Romans as a leader of the Jews. He was known for his cruelty.

DOWN:

1. King David wrote songs, recorded in the ____*Psalms*____.

2. God promised King David that *The* _____ *One* would be his descendant.

3. A man who copied the Scriptures was called a _____.

4. Solomon was known for his _____.

5. Solomon built a _____, replacing the Tabernacle.

6. When the people strayed from the Lord, God would send a _____ to warn the people.

7. Because the Israelites rejected God, he allowed them to be taken _____.

8. Satan sent _____ prophets to confuse the people.

9. With the temple destroyed as a place of worship, the Jews built _____.

10. The Jewish religious leaders, called _____, were known for being strict observers of the Law.

11. The general, Alexander the _____ brought in the influence of the Greek language and culture.

FOR FURTHER CONSIDERATION:

Find and read the following verses:

ISAIAH 29:13;   PSALM 139;   PROVERBS 1:1-7

CHAPTER TEN
REVIEW QUESTIONS

1 ELIZABETH, MARY AND JOHN

2 JESUS

3 AMONG THE SAGES

4 BAPTISM

1   ELIZABETH, MARY AND JOHN

1. The Israelites waited a long time for THE PROMISED DELIVERER to arrive. In the verse below, we see God referring to himself coming to the earth and John preparing his way as a messenger. Connect the circled words in the verse with the appropriate person or group listed below.

    | God | John | The Israelites |

    "See, I will send my messenger, who will prepare the way before me. Then suddenly the Lord you are seeking will come to his temple; the messenger of the covenant, whom you desire, will come," says the LORD Almighty.

    Malachi 3:1

2. The Bible states that THE PROMISED DELIVERER would be a descendant of King David. The prophet Jeremiah had written 600 years earlier that...

    "The days are coming," declares the Lord, "when I will raise up to David a righteous Branch, a King... This is the name by which he will be called: the LORD Our Righteousness."

    Jeremiah 23:5,6

    But because Mary and Joseph were not descendants of King David, this prophecy could not apply to their child.

    ❑   True

    ☑   False

3. The baby was called *The Son of God*.

    ☑   True

    ❑   False

4. Since Jesus was not born of a human father, he did not have Adam's sinful nature. Instead, because God was his father, he was perfect, just as God is perfect. He had God's nature.

    ☑   True

    ❑   False

5. John would be the messenger who would announce to the world the arrival of the *Lord Almighty—The Promised Deliverer*.

    ☑ True

    ❏ False

FOR FURTHER CONSIDERATION:

In Luke 1:46-55, Mary is recorded praising the Lord calling him, *"my Savior."* Mary said this, because as a sinner she knew she needed a Savior. Read these verses.

2 JESUS

1. The angel told Mary that she would bear a son, to be named J e S u S , meaning *the Lord is our deliverance*.

2. Just as God has names that depict his character, so *The Promised Deliverer* was given names that described his character. Match each name with its meaning.

    ___ A. Jesus   1. *God with us*

    ___ B. Immanuel   2. Greek for *Messiah*

    ___ C. Christ   3. *Deliverer* or *Savior*

    ___ D. Messiah   4. *Anointed One*

3. Why did Mary and Joseph have to go to Bethlehem?

    A. They had family there who wanted to see baby Jesus.

    B. Caesar was taking a census requiring everyone to go to their hometown.

    C. The leaders in Nazareth wanted to kill baby Jesus.

4. Jesus was born in Bethlehem. The town was so crowded that the only place they could find lodging was in a:

    A. stable.

    B. shepherd's field.

    C. synagogue.

5. Jesus' first visitors were a group of:

    A. learned teachers of the law.

    B. Magi.

    C. shepherds.

6. Why did Herod become upset when the Magi visited him?

    A. They were Herod's enemies.

    B. They were seeking an infant king, a threat to his reign.

    C. They had insulted him.

7. Micah and Isaiah, both prophets, had written specific details about Jesus' birth about 700 years before it happened.

    ☑ True

    ❑ False

8. What was the first thing the Magi did when they saw Jesus?

    A. They bowed down and worshiped him.

    B. They asked if Jesus was the king they were seeking.

    C. They gave Him gifts of gold, incense and myrrh.

FOR FURTHER CONSIDERATION:

1. Find and compare the following prophecies and fulfillments:

    ISAIAH 7:14; 9:6-7 ⟶ MATTHEW 1:22, 23

    MICAH 5:2   ⟶ MATTHEW 2:3-6

2. If your Bible has maps in the back, locate:

    Nazareth, Bethlehem, Jordan River, Sea of Galilee

3   AMONG THE SAGES

1. Although Jesus was God himself, he chose to come to the earth as a (an) _____.

| avatar | human | demigod |

2. At twelve, Jesus went to Jerusalem to celebrate *The Passover.*

   ☒ True

   ❏ False

3. After three days of looking, Mary and Joseph found Jesus:

   A. in the marketplace, shopping.

   B. in the streets, lost.

   Ⓒ in the Temple, in discussion with the learned men.

4. God came to earth to personally explain how man could be saved from eternal death.

   ❏ True

   ☒ False

FOR FURTHER CONSIDERATION:

Using the Concordance in the back of a Bible, find this verse by looking up the word "*flesh:*"

   *The Word became **flesh** and made his dwelling among us.*

4 BAPTISM

1. Baptism implies:

   | purity identification washing redemption |

2. To repent means to have a change of mind.

   ❏ True

   ❏ False

3. John the Baptist did not feel that the Pharisees and Sadducees needed baptism because they were already very religious.

   ❏ True

   ☒ False

4. Jesus asked John to baptize him because:

   A. he wanted to show John that he had repented.

   Ⓑ he wanted to identify John's message as being true.

   C. everyone else was being baptized.

5. When John saw Jesus coming towards him he said, *"Look, the* L A M B *of God who takes away the sins of the world."*

6. Baptism washes our sin away so we can be acceptable to God.

   ❏ True

   ☒ False

7. The Bible states that God is a tri-unity, or Trinity—the Father, Son and Spirit—but still one God. Using *IS* and *IS NOT*, complete the diagram, which assists us in our understanding of the Trinity.

IS

FATHER

GOD

IS

SON

IS

HOLY SPIRIT

FOR FURTHER CONSIDERATION:

Find and read these verses: MATTHEW 3:13-17

CHAPTER ELEVEN
REVIEW QUESTIONS

1 TEMPTED

2 POWER AND FAME

3 NICODEMUS

4 REJECTION

5 THE BREAD OF LIFE

1   TEMPTED

1. Jesus was _____ for 40 days without food.

    (A.) in a desert

    B. on a ship

    C. in prison

2. Although Jesus was God, he was also fully man, with real physical needs.

    ☑ True

    ❏ False

3. Satan tempted Jesus by suggesting that he turn the stones into bread for nourishment. If Jesus had done what Satan asked, he would have been following Satan.

    ☑ True

    ❏ False

4. Jesus countered Satan's temptation by quoting:

    A. a story he had heard.

    (B.) God's Word.

    C. his father, Joseph.

5. Jesus responded to Satan's initial challenge by stating that it was more important to be concerned about one's physical needs than to worry about one's spiritual well being.

    ❏ True

    ☑ False

6. Satan loves religion and quoting the Bible is a favorite method of deception. The Devil quoted God's Word accurately and in context when he tempted Jesus.

    ❏ True

    ☑ False

7. If Jesus worshiped Satan, he would also be serving him.

    ☑ True

    ❏ False

8. Satan succeeded in entrapping Jesus in his web of deceit.
   - ❏ True
   - ☑ False

9. The struggle between good and evil is a balanced one. Jesus is just as powerful as Satan.
   - ☑ True
   - ❏ False

10. Even those who were closest to Jesus, and most likely to know of any hidden character flaws, wrote that Jesus was _perfect_.

For Further Consideration:

Find and complete this verse:

✽ Mark 8:36 "What good is it for a man to _____ the whole _____, yet _____ his _____?"

2   Power and Fame

1. Repentance is something that happens inwardly. Jesus intended to begin his rule in the heart.
   - ☑ True
   - ❏ False

2. Jesus spoke with authority, but could not demonstrate it because he was human.
   - ❏ True
   - ☑ False

3. Jesus healed many men and women of physical handicaps and diseases because:
   - A. he felt compassion for them.
   - B. he wanted to establish that he and his message were from Heaven.
   - C. he was powerful.
   - D. he was trying to gain popularity and power among the people.

FOR FURTHER CONSIDERATION:

According to the culture of that day, a leper had to shout *"unclean"* whenever anyone approached. It was thought that if a leper was downwind, then you could approach to within 6 feet (2m), but if the leper was upwind, then not even 130 feet (40m) was safe enough. The possibility of physical contact with a leper would not only have been repulsive, but unthinkable.

Yet the Bible says that Jesus reached out his hand and deliberately touched a leper (Mark 1:40-45). That touch was not necessary. Jesus healed many a person from a distance. Think of what that touch meant to the watching crowd—to the leprous man. The event must have been electrifying! Not only was it culturally unacceptable, but according to the Law, if a man physically contacted a leper then he was ceremonially unclean. Not so with Jesus. Rather, there was the opposite effect. Jesus touched the *man* and the *leper* became clean. That touch was intentional. It was the touch of God.

3 NICODEMUS

1. Which of the following was true of Nicodemus?

    A. He was a member of the *Sanhedrin.*

    B. He was a Pharisee.

    C. He was a Jew.

    D. He was a man of status and high birth.

2. When Jesus told Nicodemus that he must be born again, Jesus was referring to a mystical and miraculous rebirth as an infant.

    ❏ True

    ☒ False

3. The Bible says that Jesus told Nicodemus that if he put his faith in Jesus, he would have <u>eTerNAL</u> life.

4. The Biblical meaning of the word *believe* can be viewed as:

    A. a simple intellectual assent.

    B. an acquiring of wisdom.

    C. synonymous with faith and trust.

    D. an abstract, mystical acquisition of knowledge.

5. The [*amount* / *object*] of one's faith is important.

6. Jesus was offering eternal life *only* to Nicodemus.

    ❏ True

    ☒ False

7. The Bible states that man is under judgment and destined for eternal death in the Lake of Fire, until he puts his trust in Jesus to deliver him.

    ☒ True

    ❏ False

8. _Jesus_ is the *light of the world*, who gives *light and life* to those who are in the darkness of sin.

FOR FURTHER CONSIDERATION:

1. Find and complete the following verses:

    ✻ JOHN 3:16-18 *"For God so* _loved_ *the world that he gave his one and only Son, that whoever* _believes_ *in him shall not* _perish_ *but have eternal* _life_*. For God did not send his son into the world to* _condemn_ *the world, but to* _save_ *the world through him. Whoever* _____ *in him is not* _____*, but whoever does* _____ *believe stands condemned* _____ *because he has not* _____ *in the name of* _____ *one and only Son."*

2. Find and read the following verses:

    JOHN 8:12   JOHN 5:24

4   REJECTION

1. When the four men couldn't reach Jesus because of the crowd, they decided to lower the paralytic through the roof.

   ☑ True

   ❏ False

2. The Bible says, "When Jesus saw their _____, he said to the paralytic, 'Son your sins are forgiven.' "

   | energy | faith | work | love |

3. Jesus showed the teachers of the law that he was God, by:

   A. forgiving sin.

   B. knowing their thoughts.

   C. healing a paralyzed man.

4. Though Levi was a Jew, he was hated by his fellow Israelites because he was a tax-collector for the Romans.

   ☑ True

   ❏ False

5. Jesus could only help those who recognized their:

   | helplessness | heritage | sinfulness | self-worth |

6. The religious leaders rejected Jesus as the Messiah because they did not want to lose their power and prestige among the people.

   ☑ True

   ❏ False

7. How many disciples did Jesus appoint?

   A. Eleven

   B. Twelve

   C. Three

8. All the disciples were educated, religious leaders.

   ❏ True

   ☒ False

FOR FURTHER CONSIDERATION:

Find and read the following verse: MATTHEW 22:15-22

5   THE BREAD OF LIFE

1. Jesus was distressed because he did not know how he and his disciples could ever feed such a large multitude.

   ❏ True

   ☒ False

2. Jesus turned a boy's lunch, which contained five small barley loaves and two small fish, into food for:

   A. 5000 men, women and children.

   B. 3000 men.

   Ⓒ 5000 men, plus women and children.

3. Those who benefited from the miracle wanted Jesus to be their _____.

God	high priest	king

4. Jesus told the crowd that their goal should be to pursue those things of eternal value.

   ☒ True

   ❏ False

5. Jesus clearly proclaimed that one must _____ in order to receive eternal life.

pray	work hard	believe

6. Jesus compared food with life. He said that he was the *Bread of* L I F E meaning only he could give eternal life.

FOR FURTHER CONSIDERATION:

Find and complete the following verse:

❋ JOHN 6:35 *Then Jesus declared, "I am the* <u>bread</u> *of* <u>life</u> *. He who comes to me will never go* _____ *, and he who* _____ *in me will never be* _____ *."*

CHAPTER TWELVE
REVIEW QUESTIONS

1 FILTHY RAGS

2 THE WAY

3 LAZARUS

4 HELL

5 ACCEPTANCE AND BETRAYAL

1 FILTHY RAGS

1. In the parable that Jesus told about the Pharisee and the tax collector, the Pharisee was relying on his own right living to make himself righteous before God.

   ☒ True

   ❏ False

2. The tax collector was conscious of the fact that he was:

   A. a helpless sinner.

   B. needing to do a multitude of good deeds to be acceptable before God.

   C. a very good and righteous man.

3. God can only work in a heart that is _____ .

repentant	proud	exalted	good

4. Jesus tied repentance to [humility / self-respect].

5. The Pharisees were relying upon which of the following to become right with God?

   A. Their religious observances.

   B. Their faith in God's mercy.

   C. Their Jewish birth.

   D. Their good works.

6. The Bible is very clear that good works is the only way one can earn a right standing with God.

   ❏ True

   ☒ False

7. The Bible says that all people are:

   A. inherently good.

   B. slaves to sin.

   C. redeemable by good works.

8. God holds everyone accountable for the choices they make.
    ☑ True
    ❏ False

FOR FURTHER CONSIDERATION:

Find and complete the following verse:

✳ ISAIAH 64:6 *All of us have become like one who is _____,*
and all our _____ acts are like ⟨filthy⟩ _____ rags;
we all shrivel up like a leaf, and like the wind our _____
sweep us away.

2 THE WAY

1. Jesus used an illustration based on:
    A. a pig pen.
    Ⓑ. a sheep pen.
    C. a cow pasture.

2. The pen had only one entrance.
    ☑ True
    ❏ False

3. In the Bible passage, John 10:7-10, Jesus likened himself to
the _____ of the sheep.

> priest   ⟨shepherd⟩   prophet   king

4. Jesus compared the things that threaten the sheep, like
thieves and wolves, to:
    A. those who steal animals.
    Ⓑ. those who proclaim another way to God.
    C. those who threaten to kill good people.

5. Just as there was only one way to gain entrance into the
sheep pen, the only way to escape the consequences of sin
is through belief in Jesus.

6. Jesus said clearly that he was the ONLY _____, the ONLY_____ and the ONLY _____.

> ~~way~~   prophet   ~~truth~~   ~~life~~   priest

FOR FURTHER CONSIDERATION:

Find and read the following verses: PROVERBS 14:12; JOHN 14:6

3 LAZARUS

1. Jesus said that the sickness and death of Lazarus would help the disciples believe.

   ❑ True

   ☒ False

2. How long was Lazarus in the tomb before Jesus arrived?

   Ⓐ 4 days

   B. 2 days

   C. Only a few hours. Jesus arrived soon after he heard.

3. Martha had faith that Jesus could raise her brother from the dead if he chose to because he was the Messiah.

   ☒ True

   ❑ False

4. Match the descriptions below with the parts of the tomb.

   _3_ A. Body

   _2_ B. Shelf on which the body was laid

   _5_ C. Trench in which the door rolled

   _1_ D. Weeping chamber

   _4_ E. Wheel-shaped rock

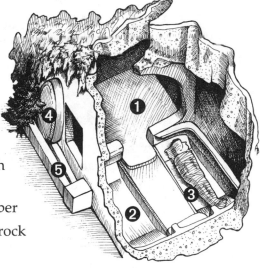

5. Though Martha knew that Lazarus would be resurrected at the end of the world, Jesus had the power to resurrect him at any moment.

    ☑ True

    ❏ False

6. Why did Jesus pray out loud when they rolled the stone away from the tomb?

    Ⓐ So those listening would believe that Jesus was God.

    B. Jesus wanted God to hear him.

    C. Jesus wanted the people to know that he was a righteous man.

7. Everyone who observed this miracle believed and followed Jesus.

    ❏ True

    ☒ False

8. The Bible clearly supports and teaches the concept of reincarnation—the belief that the dead return to this life in another body or life-form.

    ❏ True

    ☑ False

For Further Consideration:

Using the Concordance in the back of a Bible, find this verse by looking up the word "*resurrection*:"

> *Jesus said to her, "I am the **resurrection** and the life. He who believes in me will live, even though he dies…"*

4 Hell

1. Jesus told a parable about two men, a beggar and a rich man, who were judged based on their social status.

    ❏ True

    ☑ False

2. For the purposes of this study, *"Abraham's side"* is equivalent to _____ and is also referred to as *paradise*.

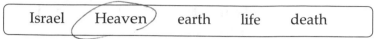

Israel   Heaven   earth   life   death

3. Why did Lazarus go to paradise?

   A. He was poor.

   B. He had faith and was coming to God in God's way.

   C. He had lived a very good life.

4. The rich man went to Hell because he ignored God and lived only for himself. There are no 2nd chances in Hell to gain Heaven. Mercy can only be received if one repents and believes during this lifetime.

second   Hell   repents   Mercy

5. The Bible says that if man refuses to believe God's written Word, then he will not be convinced even if someone is raised from the dead.

   ☒ True

   ❏ False

FOR FURTHER CONSIDERATION:

Find and read the following verses:

REVELATION 20:11-15   REVELATION 21:1-7

5 ACCEPTANCE AND BETRAYAL

1. When Jesus rode on the untrained colt through a crowd shouting *"Hosanna!"*, he was fulfilling a 500 year prophecy written by the prophet, Zechariah, which said:

   Rejoice greatly, O daughter of Zion! Shout daughter of Jerusalem! See your king comes to you, righteous and having salvation, gentle and riding on a donkey, on a colt, the foal of a donkey.   Zechariah 9:9

   ☒ True

   ❏ False

2. Hosanna means *save now*. The people were shouting this because they wanted Jesus to:

    A. forgive them and save them from eternal judgment for their sins.

    B. be their leader and overthrow the Roman oppressors.

    C. deliver them from the demands of the Pharisees.

3. Instead of leading the excited throng in rebellion, Jesus ate the Passover meal with his disciples.

    ☒ True

    ❏ False

4. Jesus discovered three days before the Passover that Judas Iscariot was a traitor.

    ❏ True

    ☒ False

5. Satan forced Judas Iscariot to betray Jesus.

    ❏ True

    ☒ False

6. Jesus said that the Passover loaf represented his b o d y .

7. Drinking of the cup was a symbol of Jesus' blood being poured out for many people.

    ❏ True

    ☒ False   *for all*

For Further Consideration:

Find and compare the following prophecies and fulfillments:

ZECHARIAH 9:9 ⟶ MARK 11:7-10

PSALMS 41:9 ⟶ MARK 14:17-20

ZECHARIAH 11:12 ⟶ MATTHEW 27:3-7

CHAPTER THIRTEEN
REVIEW QUESTIONS

1 THE ARREST

2 THE CRUCIFIXION

3 THE BURIAL AND RESURRECTION

1   THE ARREST

1. Though Jesus submitted his human will to that of his heavenly Father, he agonized over the suffering he was about to face.

    ☒ True

    ❏ False

2. When the mob, sent to arrest Jesus, told him who they were looking for, Jesus acknowledged who he was with an emphatic, "*I AM!*" A literal translation of the original language would be "*I AM right now* <u>G o d</u>."

3. These two words had little effect on the crowd around him.

    ☒ True

    ❏ False

4. When Jesus told Peter to protect him, he cut off a servant's ear.

    ☒ True

    ☒ False

5. Even in the midst of turmoil, Jesus had compassion for others.

    ☒ True

    ❏ False

6. God's questions always expose a person's true thoughts.

    ❏ True

    ❏ False

7. The night court held by the Sanhedrin was legal.

    ❏ True

    ☒ False

8. The Sanhedrin condemned Jesus to die on charges of:

    A. sedition.

    B. mutiny.

    Ⓒ blasphemy.

FOR FURTHER CONSIDERATION:

For further details of Jesus' trial before the temple officials find and read: JOHN 18:19-23

2 The Crucifixion

1. The Sanhedrin found Jesus guilty on two counts. Circle the one that was true.

    A. He opposed payment of taxes to Caesar.

    B. He claimed to be Christ / Messiah.

2. Why didn't Jesus show Herod his miracles?

    A. He had lost all his energy.

    B. Herod wanted Jesus to be a court jester—to entertain him, which showed his flagrant disrespect for who Jesus really was.

    C. He didn't want to make a spectacle of himself.

3. Isaiah 52:14 says Jesus was brutally beaten until he was disfigured beyond recognition, then mocked by the soldiers. This abuse had been recorded by Isaiah 700 years before.

    ☒ True

    ❏ False

4. *Crucifixion* was a Roman form of capital punishment used only for slaves and criminals of the lowest order.

    ☒ True

    ❏ False

5. Match the following descriptions of crucifixion with the correct picture. Circle which type Jesus was crucified upon.

    _5_ A. The victim was tacked on in various positions.

    _4_ B. The most common means apart from a tree.

    _2_ C. Hands were nailed above the head.

    _1_ D. Reserved for criminals of some notoriety.

    _3_ E. The body was nailed,with limbs at four corners.

        1   2   3   4   5

6. King David wrote about the Messiah being crucified ____ before it became Rome's official form of capital punishment.

> 200 years   800 years   50 years

7. The soldiers knew they were fulfilling an ancient prophecy as they gambled for Jesus' clothing.

    ☐ True

    ☒ False

8. Jesus assured the thief on the cross next to him that he would go to heaven, because he was putting his *faith* in Jesus to deliver him from the consequences of sin.

> belief   trust   faith   confidence

9. When Jesus died, the Temple curtain which was in front of the *Holy of Holies* was torn from top to bottom. This was significant because:

    A. no one could look behind the curtain for fear of death.

    B. the curtain was very thick and long.

    C. only God could have torn the curtain, not man.

10. The Greek word which is translated, *"It is finished,"* had many different usages during the time of Christ. Which of the following accurately expresses its meaning?

    A. The job is finished.

    B. The debt is finished.

    C. The search for an acceptable sacrifice is finished.

11. The soldiers broke Jesus' legs as requested in order to hasten his death, thus fulfilling an ancient prophecy.

    ☐ True

    ☒ False

12. All of this happened on the Day of *Pentecost* when the Passover lamb was killed.

> Preparation   Atonement   Pentecost

For Further Consideration:

Find and determine how accurate Jesus was in forecasting the details surrounding his death: Matthew 16:21; 17:22; 20:18,19

3   The Burial and Resurrection

1. Jesus was wrapped in linen and spices and laid in a tomb.

   ☑ True

   ❏ False

2. The tomb was very secure because, if a guard slept while on duty, it was punishable by death. The tomb was also:

   A. guarded by well-trained soldiers.

   B. in a remote place, a days walk from the city.

   C. sealed with the body inside.

3. When the angel of the Lord appeared in front of the tomb, what initially happened to the guards?

   A. They fought the angel.

   B. They passed out from fear.

   C. They ran away.

4. The angel told Mary and Salome that Jesus was:

dead	sleeping	alive

5. The Bible says that when John saw the empty tomb he:

fled	believed	wept	panicked

6. Jesus, *The Anointed One*, had crushed S A T A N 's head, just as God had promised back in the Garden of Eden.

7. Death is the result of sin. Jesus did not have to die, because he was sinless. He died willingly.

   ☑ True

   ❏ False

For Further Consideration:

Find and read the following verses:

John 20:26-30   Acts 2:27-32

CHAPTER FOURTEEN
REVIEW QUESTIONS

1   THE STRANGER

2   THE EMMAUS ROAD MESSAGE
— ADAM TO NOAH —

3   THE EMMAUS ROAD MESSAGE
— ABRAHAM TO THE LAW —

4   THE EMMAUS ROAD MESSAGE
— THE TABERNACLE TO THE BRAZEN SERPENT —

5   THE EMMAUS ROAD MESSAGE
— JOHN THE BAPTIST TO THE RESURRECTION —

1 THE STRANGER

1. Jesus explained to the two men that Christ had to _____.

> suffer die resurrect

2. Jesus used _____ to explain all the events surrounding his death, burial and resurrection.

   A. the Scriptures
   B. a parable
   C. the Old Testament

FOR FURTHER CONSIDERATION:

Using the Concordance in the back of a Bible, find this verse by looking up the word "*Scriptures*:"

> *And beginning with Moses and all the Prophets, he explained to them what was said in all the **Scriptures** concerning himself.*

2 THE EMMAUS ROAD MESSAGE
— ADAM TO NOAH —

1. Match the phrases below.

   ___ A. Man *chose his own path,* leading him into a spiritual wilderness.

   _3_ B. Man's *friendship* with God no longer exists.

   _5_ C. Satan *exploits* man to do his will.

   ___ D. Man joined Satan in *rebellion* against God.

   _2_ E. Sinful man is *separated relationally* from a holy God; at death, man's spirit will be *separated from his body,* and live *forever separated* from God and all future joy.

   _1_ F. Man stands in God's courtroom, *accused* of breaking his holy law.

   1. Man is *guilty.*
   2. Man is *dead.*
   3. Man is an *enemy* of God.
   4. Man is *estranged.*
   5. Man is a *slave.*
   6. Man is *lost.*

2. According to the Bible, man faces three types of death.

__2__ A. Death of the physical: 1. relationship.

__1__ B. Death to a: 2. body.

__3__ C. Death to: 3. all future joy by being confined forever in the Lake of Fire.

3. God created man with [*a will* / *emotions*] so that by his obedient choices, he would honor God.

4. Man cannot make himself acceptable to God.

    ☒ True

    ❑ False

5. Match the following to form complete sentences.

__2__ A. Just as an animal died to clothe Adam and Eve in *acceptable* clothing,

__5__ B. Just as Abel brought a *blood sacrifice* to gain forgiveness for sin,

__4__ C. Just as there was only *one* ark and *only* one door to safety,

__3__ D. Man cannot *reach* or please God through any religious effort,

__1__ E. Just as the people of Noah's day were *judged* for their sins,

1. so God will *judge* all men, regardless of their philosophy of life.

2. so Jesus died to make us *acceptable* in the presence of God.

3. but God *reached* down to man in the person of Jesus Christ.

4. so Jesus is the *only* way to eternal life.

5. so Jesus became the ultimate *blood sacrifice*, dying so that our sin might be forgiven.

6. Man had to die for his sin. But God also loved man, so, in his [*mercy* / *leniency*], he showed man [*tolerance* / *grace*]. He provided [*work* / *a way*] for man to escape that death.

7. Although we were born into this world as enemies of God, because of what Jesus did on the cross we can now be friends.

    ☒ True

    ❑ False

FOR FURTHER CONSIDERATION:

1. Find and complete the following verse:

   ✳ 1 JOHN 2:1,2 ... *Jesus Christ, the* _____
   One. He is the _____ _____
   for our _____, *and not only for ours but also for*
   the _____ *of the whole* _____.

2. Find and read the following verses:

   HEBREWS 9:22 COLOSSIANS 1:21-22 ROMANS 5:10 JOHN 14:6

3 THE EMMAUS ROAD MESSAGE
— ABRAHAM TO THE LAW —

1. Match the following to make complete sentences.

   _3_ A. Just as Isaac was bound and could not save himself,

   _2_ B. Just as the ram died in Isaac's place,

   _1_ C. Just as Abraham's sin-debt was paid when he trusted God,

   1. so Jesus pays our *sin-debt* as we put our trust in him.

   2. so Jesus died in our *place* and took our punishment on the cross. He is our substitute.

   3. so we are bound by sin and helpless to *save* ourselves from its consequences.

2. God credited righteousness to Abraham's *Certificate of Debt* because he was looking ahead to what Jesus would do on the cross.

   ☑ True

   ❑ False

3. Jesus died in our place and took our punishment for sin. He is our [*substitute* / *equal*].

4. Which statements are true in relation to the word *believe*?

   Ⓐ It is synonymous with trust, confidence and faith.

   B. It is built on fact.

   C. It involves mental assent and heart trust.

5. Jesus cried "*It is finished,*" because our sin-debt had been paid.

   ☑ True

   ❑ False

6. Match the comparisons between the *Passover* and Jesus:

_2_ A. The Passover lamb had to be *perfect*.

_5_ B. The lamb had to be a *male*.

_4_ C. The lamb died in the *place* of the first born.

_1_ D. The Israelites were not to break any *bones* of the Passover lamb.

_3_ E. When the angel of death came, he would *pass over* the house that had the blood applied.

1. None of Jesus' *bones* were broken.

2. Jesus was *sinless*.

3. God provided a way for his judgment on sin to *pass over* us. Instead the judgment came to rest on Jesus on the cross.

4. Jesus died in our *place*, as our substitute.

5. Jesus was a *man*.

7. Jesus, the *Lamb of God*, was crucified on the same day the *Passover lamb* was killed. He died at the hour the evening sacrifice was offered in the Temple.

☑ True

❏ False

8. Keeping the Ten Commandments helps us restore the broken relationship with God.

❏ True

☒ False

9. Jesus had no sin of his own to die for, so he was able to die for the sins of the whole world.

☑ True

❏ False

10. God says we are *justified*. We are [sinless / declared righteous].

11. When we are clothed in the righteousness of Christ, in God's eyes we have a *righteousness that is equal* to God's holiness.

☑ True

❏ False

12. We can only be *found righteous* by God if we put _____ in the fact that Jesus died on the cross in our place.

| faith | trust | confidence | belief |

FOR FURTHER CONSIDERATION:

1. The verse below, written hundreds of years before his birth, speaks of *The Promised Deliverer* being *our righteousness.* Find JEREMIAH 23:5-6 and complete the verse:

    "The days are coming," declares the LORD, "when I will raise up to _____ a _____ Branch, a King who will reign wisely ... This is the name by which he will be called: The _____ Our _____."

2. Find and read these verses: ROMANS 3:23; 5:1, 8-9; 4:23-24

4 THE LAW AND THE PROPHETS
— THE TABERNACLE TO THE BRAZEN SERPENT —

1. We are estranged from God because of our sin.

    ☒ True

    ❑ False

2. The animal sacrifice was a temporary payment for sin, but Jesus was the permanent and final Lamb.

    ☒ True

    ❑ False

3. The Bible says that man is *adopted* into God's family with the full rights of a son. Instead of being *estranged*, man is a *son.*

    ☒ True

    ❑ False

4. Match the following comparison of the Brazen Altar in the Tabernacle courtyard and Jesus.

The sacrifice was to be ...	Jesus ...
_3_ A. from the *herd* or the *flock.*	1. is *sinless.*
_4_ B. a *male.*	2. died in our *place.*
_1_ C. without *defect.*	3. is the *Lamb* of God.
_2_ D. accepted in man's *place.*	4. is a *male.*
_6_ E. an *atonement-covering* for his sin.	5. was the *blood sacrifice* made for us.
_5_ F. a *blood sacrifice.*	6. is our way to have *forgiveness* of sin.

5. Match the following to make complete sentences.

___1___ A. Just as the Brazen Altar was the *first step* to God through the blood sacrifice,

___2___ B. Just as the Israelite who brought an animal sacrifice was showing *faith* in God's instructions,

___4___ C. Just as the Tabernacle curtain separating man from God was torn in half, giving man *entrance* into the Holy of Holies,

___4___ D. Just as the only way for the Israelites to be healed from their snake bites was to simply *turn and look* at the bronze serpent,

1. so Jesus, our substitute Lamb, is the *first* and *only step* to having a right relationship with God.

2. so God sent Jesus to suffer as a sacrifice for man so that we might *enter* boldly into God's presence.

3. so we must put our *trust* in what Jesus did on the cross.

4. so the only way we can become right with God is to repent by simply *turning and looking* in faith to Jesus, believing that he paid our sin-debt.

6. Match the following Tabernacle furniture with the verse that compares Jesus to that object.

___4___ A. *"I am the way and the truth and the life. No one comes to the Father except through me."*   John 14:6

___1___ B. *"I am the light of the world. Whoever follows me will never walk in darkness, but will have the light of life."*   John 8:12

___2___ C. *"I tell you the truth, he who believes has everlasting life. I am the bread of life."*   John 6:47,48

___3___ D. *"Their sins and lawless acts I will remember no more." And where these have been forgiven, there is no longer any sacrifice for sin.*   Hebrews 10:17-18

1. The Lampstand

2. The Table of Bread

3. The Atonement-Cover

4. The One Gate

7. Just as Jesus rose from the grave, conquering death, so we become spiritually alive, now and for all eternity.

    ☒ True

    ❏ False

8. Although man was once spiritually dead and facing eternal death in the Lake of Fire, those who believe are now spiritually alive and will dwell forever in _He A V e N_.

FOR FURTHER CONSIDERATION:

Using a Bible, find and read the following verses:

EPHESIANS 2:4-5,13 GALATIANS 4:6-7

5 THE LAW AND THE PROPHETS
— JOHN THE BAPTIST TO THE RESURRECTION —

1. The resurrection showed that Jesus had victory over
    _ _ _ _ _; he had removed its terrible finality.

2. Match the following phrases to make complete sentences.

    ___ A. Just as a shepherd searches for and rescues his lost sheep,

    ___ B. Just as a slave was chained, helpless to deliver himself,

    ___ C. Just as there was only one door to a sheep pen,

    ___ D. Just as the Pharisees could not reach God through keeping the Ten Commandments,

    1. so we are slaves to Satan and helpless to save ourselves.

    2. so we cannot reach God through good works or deeds.

    3. so Jesus left Heaven and died on the cross for us, in our place, to pay our sin-debt in order to rescue us from death.

    4. so there is only one way to God.

3. Who is responsible for the death of Jesus on the cross?

    A. Just the Jewish nation

    B. The Roman soldiers alone

    C. The whole world

4. On the cross, there was a great exchange. Jesus took our
   _____ and gave us his _____.

   > faith   sin   confidence   righteousness   love

5. Salvation is a _ _ _ _ from God, not an *award*. We cannot earn it and we do not deserve it.

6. It is not the size of our faith, but in [*whom / what*] we are placing our faith that is significant.

7. By _ _ _ _ _,

   We *believe* that Jesus died in our place for our sin.

   We *believe* that Jesus paid our sin-debt.

   We *believe* that God's justice was satisfied by Jesus' death.

   We *believe* that God gives us the gift of eternal life.

8. Circle the reasons why Jesus died.

   A. Our sin demanded death.

   B. Jesus had to die for his own sin.

   C. Jesus took the eternal consequences of our sin upon himself.

For Further Consideration:

Find and read the following verses:

John 3:16, 18   2 Corinthians 5:21   Ephesians 1:7-9

Acts 4:12   Hebrews 2:14,15

CHAPTER FIFTEEN
REVIEW QUESTIONS

1   WHAT DO YOU WANT ME TO DO?

2   A CONVENIENT TIME

1 WHAT DO YOU WANT ME TO DO?

1. The Bible says Jesus is coming a second time. We can be sure that this will happen because God always keeps his promises.

    ❏ True

    ❏ False

2. Saul was known among followers of Jesus:

    A. as a righteous man.

    B. as the apostles' first convert.

    C. as a feared persecutor of the followers of Jesus.

3. When Saul heard God's voice from Heaven on the way to Damascus, he refused to stop persecuting the believers.

    ❏ True

    ❏ False

4. The Bible says that if we reject the message of the cross:

    A. we can find other ways to God.

    B. there will be more chances to choose otherwise.

    C. the rest of *Scripture* will not be understood correctly because it is veiled to those who are perishing.

5. The Bible says that because you are a sinner, you have a sin-debt that you must forever pay—a debt that requires separation from God in the Lake of Fire. It also says that if you believe Jesus paid your sin-debt, and you trust in Him alone to deliver you from sin's penalty, then God forgives your sin, and your relationship with God is restored.

    ❏ True

    ❏ False

6. If you have put your trust in Jesus Christ, the Bible says that your *Certificate of Debt* was nailed to the cross two thousand years ago, removing your sin-debt.

    ❏ True

    ❏ False

7. Connect the following icons through the cross.

A. DEBTOR

B. GUILTY

C. ETERNAL JUDGEMENT

D. SLAVE

E. STRANGER

F. ENEMY

G. LOST

1. FOUND

2. SET-FREE REDEEMED

3. RECONCILED

4. ADOPTED

5. DECLARED RIGHTEOUS

6. ETERNAL LIFE

7. CANCELED DEBT

8. God forgives us assuming we will live sin-free lives.

❏ True

❏ False

9. A believer relates to God in much the same way a son relates to his father. His [*fellowship / relationship*] with his father is fixed. They will always be father and son. However, if the son disobeys, then his [*fellowship / relationship*] with his father is broken until he admits his guilt and asks forgiveness.

10. The Scripture says that the life a person lives is determined by the [*goodness / focus*] he maintains.

11. Using a Bible, find the following verses and identify the word that is synonymous with the word *focus.*

    COLOSSIANS 3:1-2   *Since, then, you have been raised with Christ, _____ your hearts on things above, where Christ is seated at the right hand of God. _____ your minds on things above, not on earthly things.*

    HEBREWS 12:2   *Let us _____ our eyes on Jesus, the author and perfecter of our faith, who for the joy set before him endured the cross, scorning its shame, and sat down at the right hand of the throne of God.*

    HEBREWS 3:1   *Therefore, holy brothers, who share in the heavenly calling, _____ your thoughts on Jesus, the apostle and high priest whom we confess.*

    2 PETER 3:12   *... as you _____ _____ to the day of God and speed its coming.*

12. What are the things we are to focus on?

    A. What we now have because of Jesus

    B. Getting better acquainted with Jesus

    C. Trusting him with everything

    D. Ourselves and our well-being

13. Which of the following are considered *enemies*—things that destroy our focus?

    A. Our human nature

    B. The world system

    C. The Devil

14. Our human nature has an in-built desire to focus on:

   A. God.

   B. others.

   C. ourselves.

15. Obsession with _____, its needs and desires, is always harmful. We find true joy when we become caught up in knowing ____and serving _____.

   | others   self   God |

16. We grow strong spiritual roots as we keep our _ _ _ _ _ _.

17. There are several things that would help us grow spiritually by maintaining our focus. Match the following:

   ___ A. God himself   1. Helps encourage us.

   ___ B. By faith   2. The disciples went all over, *sharing* this good news.

   ___ C. The Bible   3. We gain spiritual maturity through these friendships.

   ___ D. Prayer   4. Some day, Jesus will return.

   ___ E. Telling others   5. This is how we *walk* with God.

   ___ F. Music   6. Simply talking to God.

   ___ G. Other believers   7. Indwells us in the person of the *Holy Spirit*.

   ___ H. Future hope   8. It is a source of daily strength.

FOR FURTHER CONSIDERATION:

Find and read the following verses:

   TITUS 2:11-14   COLOSSIANS 2:13,15   PSALMS 103:11,12

   JOHN 14:1-41   THESSALONIANS 4:13-18   HEBREWS 12:1,2

2   A CONVENIENT TIME

1. Why did Herod die?

    A. He eventually contracted a fatal illness.

    B. He didn't trust God and give him glory and praise.

    C. One of his bodyguards killed him while he was in a drunken stupor.

2. According to the Bible, God in his *grace* will tolerate sin for awhile, but then in his *justice* he will judge it—either in this life or after death.

    ❏ True

    ❏ False

3. After hearing the message about Jesus from Paul, Felix said he wanted to wait for a more convenient time.

    ❏ True

    ❏ False

FOR FURTHER CONSIDERATION:

Find and read the following verse: 2 CORINTHIANS 6:2

ANSWERS
TO THE
QUESTIONS

ANSWERS FOR CHAPTER ONE

1 PROLOGUE

No questions

2 GETTING THINGS STRAIGHT

1. *True*   (page 6)
2. *True*   (page 7)
3. *A, B, C, D*   (pages 7-8)
4. *B*   (page 8)
5. *A, B, D.* In such a short book, it is not possible to give one an extensive, comprehensive understanding of the Bible.   (page 7,8)

3 A UNIQUE BOOK

1. *C*   (page 9)
2. *B*   (page 9)
3. *C*   (page 9)
4. *B*   (page 10)
5. *A*   (page 10)
6. *False.* It is true that God guided the prophets, that what was recorded was precisely what he wanted written, but these men were not free to add their own private thoughts.   (page 10)
7. *A*   (page 12)
8. *False.* The concordance is a Bible navigational aid. (page 12)
9. *B*   (page 12)

ANSWERS FOR CHAPTER TWO

1 IN THE BEGINNING GOD...

1. *False.* The Bible says God had no beginning and will have no end—he is eternal. (page 15)
2. *everlasting* (page 15)
3. *C* (page 18)
4. *I Am* (page 18)
5. *True* (page 18)
6. *False.* There is no other God. He stands alone as the ruler of the Universe. (pages 18-19)
7. *A, B, C* (page 18-19)
8. *One* (page 19)
9. *Spirit* (pages 19-20)

2 ANGELS, HOSTS, AND STARS

1. *A, B, C, D* (page 20)
2. *A, B* (page 21)
3. *True* (page 21)
4. He who *creates* the paddle, also *owns* the paddle. (page 21)
5. *False.* Angelic beings were originally created with the ability to choose. (page 22)
6. *B* (page 22)
7. *True* (page 22)
8. *A* (page 23)
9. *Worth* (page 23)

ANSWERS FOR CHAPTER THREE

1 HEAVEN AND EARTH

1. *True* (page 25)
2. *B* (page 28)
3. *Nothing* (page 25)
4. *True* (page 26)
5. *False.* God knows everything. (page 25)
6. A. All-*knowing*
   B. All-*powerful*
   C. Everywhere present at *one time* (page 26)
7. *False.* The Bible clearly teaches that God is *greater than* and *separate from* his creation. (page 29)

2 IT WAS GOOD

1. *False.* God created everything in six days. (page 30)
2. *True* (page 30)
3. *Order* (page 32)
4. *True* (page 33)
5. *Kind* (page 34)
6. *A, B, C* (pages 34-35)
7. *Righteous, Holy* (page 35)
8. *Cares, Loves* (pages 35-36)

FOR FURTHER CONSIDERATION:

_g_ Day One   _f_ Day Four   _d_ Day Six
_e_ Day Two   _b_ Day Five   _c_ Day Seven
_a_ Day Three

3 MAN AND WOMAN

1. *A, C, D* (pages 37-38)
2. *A* (page 38)
3. *B* (page 39)
4. *B* (page 39)
5. *False.* Because God was Adam and Eve's Creator-Owner, he did not consult with them. He knew what was best. (page 40)
6. *Owner* (page 40)
7. *B* (page 40-41)
8. *Choose* (page 41)
9. *C* (page 41)
10. *True* (page 41)
11. *A* (page 42-43)
12. *True* (page 42)

FOR FURTHER CONSIDERATION:

The concordance should lead you to GENESIS 1:27

ANSWERS FOR CHAPTER FOUR

1 I WILL

1. *B*   (page 47)
2. *I will, I will, I will, I will, I will*   (page 48)
3. *Pride*   (page 48)
4. *Sin*   (page 48)
5. *Sin*   (page 49)
6. *True*   (page 50)
7. *B*   (page 49)
8. A: *b, c*   B: *a, d*   (page 50)
9. *Lake* of *Fire*   (page 50)

2 HAS GOD SAID

1. *A*   (page 51)
2. *B*   (page 52)
3. *A*   (page 53)
4. *Better than, better than* (page 54)
5. *False*. God considers all disobedience to be sin. (page 55)
6. *True*   (page 55)
7. *Guilt or Shame*   (page 55)
8. *Choice; sin*   (page 57, inside box)
9. *False*. God is holy and therefore cannot tolerate sin in His presence. Adam and Eve's disobedience opened a vast gulf in the relationship between God and man.(page 55)

3 WHERE ARE YOU?

1. *True*   (page 58)
2. *Question*   (page 58)
3. *True*   (page 58)
4. *A, B*   (page 59)
5. *B, D*   (page 59)
6. *False*. They never admitted to being wrong about their sin. (page 59)
7. *B*   (page 60)
8. *A, B, C*   (pages 60-61)
9. *A*   (page 60)
10. *True*   (page 61)
11. *B*   (page 61)
12. *Death*   (page 61)

4 DEATH

1. *False*   (page 62)
2. A: *3* B: *1* C: 2   (pages 62-65, Headings)
3. *True*   (page 65)

Crossword Puzzle answers are found on pages 62-68.

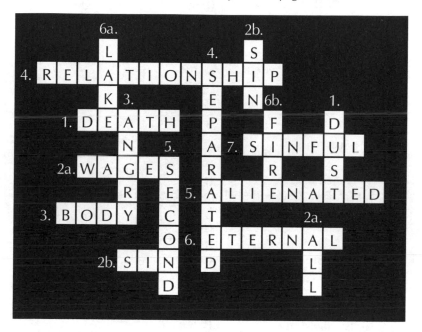

Answers For Chapter Five

1 A Paradox

1. *Laws*   (page 71)
2. *Certificate* of *Debt*   (page 71)
3. The law of *sin* and *death*.   (page 71)
4. *True*   (page 71)
5. *B*   (page 71)
6. *sin, perfection* or *righteousness* (page 72)
7. *True*   (page 72)
8. *care* and *concern; undeserved* (page 73)
9. *All*   (page 73)
10. *A*   (page 74)
11. *A*   (page 74)

2 Atonement

1. *Remove*   (page 74)
2. *Death*   (page 75)
3. *False.* Cain and Abel inherited Adam's sin nature. (page 76)
4. *B*   (page 76)
5. *C*   (page 77)
6. *A*   (page 77)
7. *Covering*   (page 77)
8. *A, B, C*   (page 77)
9. 1. *faith* or *trust*
   2. *God's*   (page 79)
10. *Blood*   (page 79)
11. *Abel*   (page 80)
12. *Death*   (page 82)
13. *Life*   (page 82)

3 Two by Two

1. *Deliverer*   (page 84)
2. *False.* All but a few turned their backs on God. (page 84)
3. *C*   (page 86)
4. *C*   (page 85)
5. *True*   (page 86)
6. *A, B, C*   (pages 86)
7. *Death*   (page 86)
8. *Door*   (page 87)
9. *False.* God shut the door.   (page 88)
10. *True*   (page 89)
11. *True*   (page 90)
12. *B*   (page 92)

For further consideration:

The Concordance should lead you to Genesis 7:5

4 BABEL

1. *False.* God had commanded them to fill the earth. (page 94)
2. *C*   (page 95)
3. *False*   (page 95)
4. *Religion*   (page 95)
5. *Religion*   (page 96)
6. *True*   (page 96)
7. *A, B, C*   (pages 76-77)
8. *True*   (page 97)

ANSWERS FOR CHAPTER SIX

1 ABRAHAM

1. *A, B, C*   (page 101)
2. *B*   (page 102)
3. *True*   (page 102)
4. God said that because of Abram's *confidence* in God, righteousness was *credited to* Abram's account offsetting his *sin-debt.*   (page 103)
5. *B*   (page 104)
6. *True*   (page 104)

2 BELIEF

1. *Trust*   (page 104)
2. *A*   (page 104)
3. *True*   (page 105)
4. It's not the *amount* of faith you have, but in *whom* you are placing your faith.   (page 105)
5. *False.* Because Abram trusted God, the natural result was that he did the things God wanted him to do.   (page 105)

3 ISAAC

1. *B*   (page 108)
2. *True*   (page 108)
3. *A*   (page 109)
4. *True*   (page 110)
5. *C*   (page 111)
6. *C*   (page 111)
7. A: *3* B: *1* C: *5* D: *4* E: *2* (page 111)
8. *False.* It was God's idea.   (page 111)
9. *True*   (page 111)

Answers for Chapter Seven

1 Israel and Judah

1. *A*   (page 113)
2. *Deliverer*   (page 113)
3. *False.* Jacob had 13 children—12 sons and one daughter, but only 12 tribes descended from the sons. (page 113)
4. *True*   (page 113)
5. *True*   (page 113)
6. *C*   (page 114)

2 Moses

1. *C*   (page 114)
2. *True*   (page 116)
3. *B*   (page 116)
4. *C*   (page 116)
5. *False.* They believed, just as God promised. (page 117)

For further consideration:

The Concordance should lead you to Exodus 3:14-15

3 Pharaoh and the Passover

1. *A*   (pages 117-118)
2. *False.* Instead, they were to be an example of how God relates to mankind. (page 118)
3. *A* and *B*   (page 118)
4. *True*   (page 119)
5. *way*   (page 120)
6. *False.* God gave specific instructions to the Israelites and made it clear that they were to be obeyed. (page 122)
7. *True*   (page 122)
8. *True*   (page 123)
9. A: *3*   B: *1*   C: *2*   (page 123)

ANSWERS FOR CHAPTER EIGHT

1 BREAD, QUAIL AND WATER

1. *False.* They grumbled and complained.   (page 125)
2. *A, B, D*   (pages 126-127)
3. *B*   (page 126)
4. *False*   (page 126)
5. *False.* He provided daily and abundantly.   (page 126)
6. *Merciful, gracious, kind; obeyed, trusted*   (pages 126-127)
7. *True*   (page 127)

2 TEN RULES

1. *Obey*   (page 128)
2. *False.* They felt confident that they could do what God required.   (page 129)
3. *Purity of lifestyle*   (page 129)
4. *C*   (page 129)
5. *True*   (page 130)
6. *B*   (page 131)
7. *True*   (page 131)
8. *Honor*   (page 132)
9. *Murder*   (pages 132-133)
10. *A, B, C*   (page 133)
11. *Lies*   (page 134)
12. *True*   (page 134)
13. *False.* We can **always** count on it being true. (page 134)
14. *False.* God's expectations have remained constant and unchanging.   (page 135)
15. *True*   (page 135)

3 THE COURTROOM

1. *C*   (pages 135-136)
2. *True*   (page 136)
3. *False.* We are incapable of keeping the law consistently and perfectly.   (page 136)
4. *A, B*   (page 137)
5. *sin*   (page 137)
6. *B*   (page 138)
7. *A*   (page 138)
8. *C*   (page 139)
9. *True*   (page 141)

ANSWERS FOR CHAPTER NINE

1 TABERNACLE

1. *Helpless* (page 143)
2. *False*. They were to follow God's explicit instructions. (page 144)
3. *True* (page 145)
4. *C* (page 145)
5. A: *CY* B: *HH* C: *CY* D: *HP* E: *HP* F: *HH* G: *HP* (pages 146-147)
6. *True* (page 148)
7. . *True* (page 150)
8. *A, B, C, D, E* (page 150)
9. *C* (page 150)
10. *hands; head; substitute* (page 150)
11. *A* (page 151)
12. Aaron, the High Priest, entered the Holy of Holies once a year—never without **blood** which he offered on the **Atonement Cover**. This was done on the Day of Atonement. (page 152)

2 UNBELIEF

1. *accountable* (page 153)
2. *False*. They grumbled and complained again. (page 153)
3. *True*. (page 153)
4. *B* (page 154)
5. *Death* (page 154)
6. *Repent* (page 154)
7. *True* (page 154
8. *B* (page 155)
9. *False*. It was simply an opportunity for the Israelites to show they trusted God. (page 155)

3 JUDGES, KINGS AND PROPHETS

<u>2</u> Enslaved
<u>3</u> Repent
<u>1</u> Rebel
<u>4</u> Delivered

(page 156)

Crossword Puzzle answers are on pages 156-161.

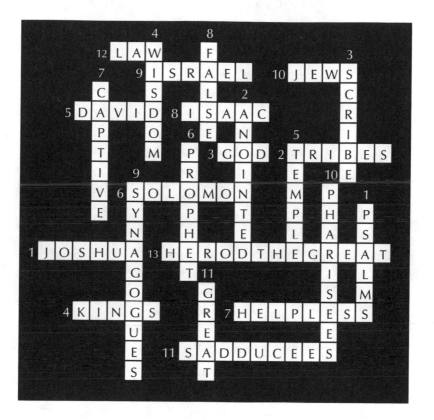

Answers for Chapter Ten

1 Elizabeth, Mary and John

1.

   | God | | John | | The Israelites |

"See, I will send my messenger, who will prepare the way before me. Then suddenly the Lord you are seeking will come to his temple; the messenger of the covenant, whom you desire, will come," says the LORD Almighty. (page 166)

2. *False.* Mary and Joseph were direct descendants of David. (page 167)
3. *True* (page 167)
4. *True* (page 168)
5. *True* (page 168)

2 Jesus

1. *Jesus* (page 170)
2. A: *3* B: *1* C: *2* D: *4* (pages 170-171, 173)
3. *B* (page 171)
4. *A* (page 172)
5. *C* (page 172)
6. *B* (page 174)
7. *True* (pages 171, 174)
8. *A* (page 175)

3 Among the Sages

1. *Human* (*avatar* and *demigod* are incorrect) (page 177)
2. *True* (page 177)
3. *C* (page 178)
4. *True* (page 169)

For further consideration:

The Concordance should lead you to John 1:14.

4 Baptism

1. *Identification* (page 180)
2. *True* (page 180)
3. *False.* He called them hypocrites because, though they were sinful, they thought themselves righteous. (page 181)
4. *B* (page 181)
5. *Lamb* (page 181)
6. *False.* It neither removes sin or makes us acceptable with God. (page 182)
7. (page 185)

Answers For Chapter Eleven

1 Tempted

1. *A* (page 187)
2. *True* (page 187)
3. *True* (page 187)
4. *B* (page 187)
5. *False.* Jesus said man's primary concern should be his spiritual well being. (page 187)
6. *False.* Satan always misquotes scripture. (page 188)
7. *True* (page 188)
8. *False.* Jesus was above reproach. (page 189)
9. *False.* Jesus, the Creator God, is far more powerful than Satan, a created being. (page 189)
10. *Sinless* or *perfect*. (page 189)

2 Power and Fame

1. *True* (page 190)
2. *False.* Jesus was God and gave his words credibility through his actions. (page 191)
3. *A, B, C* (page 191)

3 Nicodemus

1. *A, B, C, D* (page 192)
2. *False.* He was referring to a spiritual rebirth. (page 192)
3. *Eternal* (page 193)
4. *C* (page 193)
5. The *object* of one's faith is important. (page 193)
6. *False.* Jesus offered eternal life to *everyone*. (page 193)
7. *True* (page 194)
8. *Jesus* (page 194)

4 Rejection

1. *True* (page 195)
2. *Faith* (page 195)
3. *A, B, C* (page 196)
4. *True* (page 197)
5. *Helplessness; sinfulness* (page 197)
6. *True* (page 198)
7. *B* (page 199)
8. *False.* None of the disciples were religious leaders. (page 199)

5 The Bread of Life

1. *False.* Jesus could do anything. (page 199)
2. *C* (page 200)
3. *King* (page 200)
4. *True* (page 201)
5. *Believe* (page 201)
6. *Life* (page 201)

Answers for Chapter Twelve

1 Filthy Rags

1. *True*   (page 203)
2. *A*   (page 203)
3. *Repentant*   (page 204)
4. *Humility*   (page 204)
5. *A, C, D*   (page 204)
6. *False.* The Bible is clear that good deeds **cannot** earn a right standing with God   (page 205)
7. *B*   (page 205)
8. *True*   (page 205)

2 The Way

1. *B*   (page 206)
2. *True*   (page 206)
3. *Shepherd*   (page 207)
4. *B*   (page 207)
5. *Jesus*   (page 208)
6. *Way, truth, life*   (page 208)

3 Lazarus

1. *True*   (page 208)
2. *A*   (page 209)
3. *True*   (page 209)
4. *A: 3   B: 2   C: 5   D: 1   E: 4* (page 210)
5. *True*   (page 209)
6. *A*   (page 210)
7. *False.* A few believed, but many turned and plotted against him.   (page 211)
8. *False.* The Bible teaches that man dies only once and never returns to live again on earth. Reincarnation is not taught as truth anywhere in the Bible.   (page 211)

For further consideration:

The Concordance should lead you to John 11:25

4 Hell

1. *False.* They were judged by whether they trusted God or not.   (page 212)
2. *Heaven*   (page 212)
3. *B*   (page 212)
4. The rich man went to *hell* because he ignored God and lived only for himself. There are no *second* chances in Hell to gain Heaven. *Mercy* can only be received if one *repents* and believes during this lifetime. (page 212-213)
5. *True*   (page 213)

5 Acceptance and Betrayal

1. *True* (page 214)
2. *B* (page 214)
3. *True* (page 215)
4. *False.* He knew when he chose Judas as a disciple. (page 215)
5. *False.* Judas had a will and chose to betray Jesus. (page 215)
6. *Body* (page 216)
7. *True* (page 216)

Answers for Chapter Thirteen

1 The arrest

1. *True* (page 219)
2. *God* (page 220)
3. *False.* When Jesus spoke the words *"I AM,"* the mob *"drew back and fell to the ground."* (page 220)
4. *False.* Though it is true that Peter did cut off the servant's ear, Jesus did not tell Peter to protect him. (page 220)
5. *True* (page 220)
6. *True* (page 221)
7. *False.* Night courts were illegal. (page 221)
8. *C* (page 222)

2 the crucifixion

1. *B* (page 222)
2. *B* (page 225)
3. *True* (page 227)
4. *True* (page 228)
5. A: *1* B: *4* C: *2* D: *5* E: *3* (page 229)
6. *800 years* (page 229)
7. *False.* The soldiers had no idea they were fulfilling an ancient prophecy. (page 230)
8. *All are correct* (page 231)
9. *A, B, C* (page 232)
10. *A, B, C* (pages 233-234)
11. *False.* Jesus' bones were not broken. (page 234)
12. *Preparation* (page 228)

3 The Burial and Resurrection

1. *True* (page 235)
2. *A, C* (page 236)
3. *B* (pages 236-237)
4. *Alive* (page 237)
5. *Believed* (page 238)
6. *Satan* (page 240)
7. *True* (pages 241)

ANSWERS FOR CHAPTER FOURTEEN

1 THE EMMAUS ROAD MESSAGE

1. *Suffer, die, resurrect*   (page 244)
2. *A* and *C*   (pages 244-245)

FOR FURTHER CONSIDERATION:

The Concordance should lead you to Luke 24:27.

2 THE EMMAUS ROAD MESSAGE
— ADAM TO NOAH —

1. A: *6* B: *4* C: *5* D: *3* E: *2* F: *1*   (pages 246-247)
2. A: *2* B: *1* C: *3*   (page 247)
3. God created man with *a will*, so that by his obedient choices, he would honor God.   (page 246)
4. *True*   (page 248)
5. A: *2* B: *5* C: *4* D: *3* E: *1*   (pages 248-252)
6. Man had to die for his sin. But God also loved man, so, in his *mercy*, he showed man *grace*. He provided *a way* for man to escape that death.   (page 248)
7. *True*   (page 250)

3 THE EMMAUS ROAD MESSAGE
— ABRAHAM TO THE LAW —

1. A: *3* B: *2* C: *1*   (page 252-253)
2. *True*   (page 253)
3. Jesus died in our place and took our punishment for sin; he is our *substitute*.   (page 253)
4. *A, B, C*   (page 254)
5. *True*   (page 254)
6. A: *2* B: *5* C: *4* D: *1* E: *3*   (page 255)
7. *True*   (page 256)
8. *False.* The Ten Commandments show us that we are sinners who can only come to God in God's way.   (page 256)
9. *True*   (page 258)
10. God says we are *justified* or *declared righteous.* (page 258)
11. *True*   (page 258)
12. *All are correct*   (pages 258-259)

4 THE EMMAUS ROAD MESSAGE
— THE TABERNACLE TO THE BRAZEN SERPENT —

1. *True*   (page 262)
2. *True*   (page 263)
3. *True*   (page 262)
4. A: *3* B: *4* C: *1* D: *2* E: *6* F: *5*   (page 260)
5. A: *1* B: *3* C: *2* D: *4*   (pages 260-264)
6. A: *4* B: *1* C: *2* D: *3*   (pages 260-261, 263)
7. *True*   (page 264)
8. *Heaven*   (page 264)

5 THE EMMAUS ROAD MESSAGE
— JOHN THE BAPTIST TO THE RESURRECTION —

1. *Death*   (page 267)
2. A: *3* B: *1* C: *4* D: *2*   (pages 265, 268-270)
3. *C*   (page 267)
4. *Sin*   (page 266)
5. *Gift*   (page 271)
6. *Whom*   (page 272)
7. *Faith*   (page 271)
8. *A* and *C*   (page 273)

ANSWERS FOR CHAPTER FIFTEEN

1 WHAT DO YOU WANT ME TO DO?

1. *True*   (page 275)
2. *C*   (page 275)
3. *False*. He did believe and became a strong leader among the believers.   (page 276)
4. *C*   (page 277)
5. *True*   (page 277)
6. *True*   (page 280)
7. A: *7* B: *5* C: *6* D: *2* E: *4* F: *3* G: *1* (pages 278-279)
8. *False*. If we are trusting in God, His forgiveness is unconditional and total.   (page 281)
9. A believer relates to God in much the same way as a son relates to his father. His *relationship* with his father is fixed. They will always be father and son. However, if the son disobeys, then his *fellowship* with his father is broken until he admits his guilt and asks forgiveness.   (page 282)
10. The Scripture says that the life a person lives is determined by the *focus* he maintains.   (page 282)
11. *set; set; fix; fix; look forward*
12. *A, B, C*   (pages 282-283)
13. *A, B, C*   (pages 284-285)
14. *C*   (page 284)
15. *self; God; others*   (page 284)
16. *focus*   (page 285)
17. A: *7* B: *5* C: *8* D: *6* E: *2* F: *1* G: *3* H: *4* (pages 286-290)

2 A CONVENIENT TIME

1. *B*   (page 291)
2. *True*   (page 291)
3. *True*   (page 292)

The companion volume to the *WorkBook*.

This book is directed at those who would consider themselves biblical novices, though many with a Bible background will profit from its reading. As a narrative, the Bible is explained chronologically from the beginning to the end, starting with the simple and moving to the complex. The goal is to make the Bible's message clear and logical.

ISBN: 978-1-890082-54-3

Also as an AudioBook, DVD series and in various translations.

CALL TO ORDER

GoodSeed Australia
1800 897-333
info.au@goodseed.com

GoodSeed Canada
800 442-7333
info.ca@goodseed.com

BonneSemence Canada
Service en français
888 314-3623
info.qc@goodseed.com

GoodSeed Europe
info.eu@goodseed.com

GoodSeed UK
0800 073-6340
info.uk@goodseed.com

GoodSeed USA
888 654-7333
info.us@goodseed.com

GoodSeed® International

P. O. Box 3704
Olds, AB T4H 1P5
CANADA
Business: 403 556-9955
Facsimile: 403 556-9950
Email: info@goodseed.com

goodseed
see·hear·understand
—— www.goodseed.com ——

'GoodSeed,' and the Book/Leaf design mark are trademarks of GoodSeed International.